Barking Sycamores:
Year One

Edited by V. Solomon Maday and N.I. Nicholson

Owned by disabled workers, NeuroQueer Books extends the Autonomous Press mission: Revolutionizing academic access

Autonomous Press is an independent publisher focusing on works about disability, neurodivergence, and the various ways they can intersect with other aspects of identity and lived experience.

ISBN-10: 0-9972971-0-7

ISBN-13: 978-0-9972971-0-2

Cover art by N.I. Nicholson, Samm Almester, and Barbara Ruth (whose works are also in this anthology).

Barking Sycamores is a quarterly literary journal whose mission is to publish poetry, short fiction, creative nonfiction, hybrid genre work, and artwork by neurodivergent authors. Recent issues are available online at **http://barkingsycamores.wordpress.com.**

Table of Contents

Issue 2: Summer/Fall 2014 (If Thine Eye be Single) – *(63)*

Poetry

Artwork

Issue 3: Fall/Winter 2014 – *(115)*

Poetry and Short Fiction

Issue 4: Winter/Spring 2015 – *(155)*

Poetry and Short Fiction

Artwork

Contributors – *(190)*

Introduction

Wow.

Normally as verbose as we are, we at *Barking Sycamores* become speechless sometimes when we think about the very fact of this *Year One* anthology even becoming a reality.

We initially began as an online journal, emerging in the spring of 2014 and opening our doors to poetry and artwork submissions; later, beginning with Issue 3, we welcomed short fiction into our journal. With the help of individual neurodivergent folk, online neuroqueer communities, organizations such as *Awe In* Autism and *The Art of Autism*, and MFA/Creative Writing/English programs around the United States, word spread about *Barking Sycamores*. Within the first two issues' reading periods we pretty quickly found ourselves inundated in submissions —a *good* problem to have.

From the beginning, we desired to publish a print edition of the journal. However, we found ourselves with the zeal but without the budget to do so. In the summer of 2014, Autonomous Press approached us and offered to help make this happen. So here we are, with our first year's collection of issues: the work you hold in your hands, whether as a printed book or on a digital device, is a testament to not only the burgeoning genre of neurodivergent literature and art but also Autonomous' belief in our little journal.

As we approach the end of our second year of publishing online, we're absolutely thrilled to be able to offer this collection of our first four issues in print. Not bad for a couple of loudmouthed autistic geeks from the Midwest, eh? Of course, there is *no way* any of this would have happened without: Autonomous Press; the creatives who allowed us to publish their work in the first four issues; the support we received from friends and fellow activists; the Divine's presence which supported us through the launch and operations of the journal; and you, the reader, who kept coming back every Tuesday, Thursday, and Saturday during each issue to read new work.

We look forward to an amazing future. Keep barking, friends. You all are *brilliant.*

Allons-y!

V. Solomon Maday
N.I. Nicholson
Grove City, Ohio

Works Not Included in This Anthology

Nearly all of the poems, short fiction pieces, and artwork which appeared in the first four issues of *Barking Sycamores* also appear in this collection. However, as we were unable to contact some of the authors while compiling this anthology, we opted not to include their works. While we do ask authors to grant us non-exclusive anthology rights when we accept their work for initial publication on the journal's website, we felt that the best ethical option in the cases of the authors we could not contact was not to publish their work in print without their knowledge. Should we hear from these authors at a later time, we may consider other options to bring their work to print.

The following works were originally published in the journal online, but do not appear in this printed collection:

- "Untitled" by Calmen Clement (Artwork, Issue 1)
- "Civil Disobedience," "Pendant," and "Snowfall" by Beebe Barksdale-Bruner

BARKING SYCAMORES

Issue 1: Spring/Summer 2014

(Cover Art: N.I. Nicholson)

Introduction: Issue 1

Morning has broken, like the first morning,
Blackbird has spoken, like the first bird.
Praise for the singing, praise for the morning,
Praise for them springing fresh from the word.
— Elaine Farjeon

Welcome, friends, to issue #1 of *Barking Sycamores*. Morning has broken for us, and we greet this new day with hope, optimism, and a mission.

The desire to communicate is as natural as breathing. We can't exist on this planet for any length of time and not desire to express *something* about ourselves — whether to our loved ones, a friend, a neighbor, the world at large, the trees, a passing shaft of light, whatever we perceive as the Divine, or even within our own psyches which are themselves the sum of many processes, aspects, and functional areas inside us. The visual, musical, and literary arts are all forms of communication; indeed, it is through these mediums that many of us communicate messages and meaning not adequately conveyed through speech alone.

The neurodivergent — those of us who are wired differently than the currently perceived neurological "norms" — have been negotiating a world not built for us for our entire existences. In our journeys we, too, find that we have a need to communicate; and for those of us who communicate artistically, these mediums are ways in which we give ourselves a voice, especially when speech is inaccessible or just simply not enough. As one of the poets and artists in this issue, Kimberly Gerry Tucker, said when interviewed for her feature on the *Awe in Autism* website:

Artistic expression is an important, even therapeutic means of communication — to be able to "go to another place" for a while, especially since I struggle with effective communication. When I saw the movie *The King's Speech*, my eyes stung with tears again and again. I related deeply to the main character's humility, fear, anger, embarrassment, and frustration at not having a reliable voice in expected situations.

Sometimes, these acts of artistic communication are met with surprise and disbelief. For example, some of us who are autistic have difficulties with speech communication or do not communicate by speech at all — but an overemphasis on these difficulties with verbal communication has promoted a severely limited idea of how autistic people can and do communicate. In addition, the easy dismissal of some manifestations of autistic communication (such as echolalia and hyperlexia) as being without function or meaning have created an assumption that autistic artistic communication does not exist — or if it does, it is either an unlikely fluke, a savant ability, simple imitation, or meaningless gibberish.

For those of us who are other forms of neurodivergent (such as AD(H)D and bipolar) there can also be a reticence to understand our artistic communication. This is often based on the assumption that our messages cannot be understood or are inaccessible to the common public (if such a thing as "the common public" really does exist) because they do not share our neurodivergent realities. Even worse is dismissal of our artistic communication as nothing but products of genius, madness, or a liminal space between the two without any further attempt to glean meaning from or understand the humanity within them.

We, the editors, know of course how false these assumptions are. Both of us are autistic and have been communicating ourselves through art since we were children — N.I. as writer and visual artist, and Solomon as musician and writer. And after their autism diagnosis in 2010, N.I. began a journey of trying to understand autism and their own autistic nature; along the way, N.I. has met many autistic writers, musicians, and visual artists who gave voice to unique visions and ways of seeing, feeling, and being.

Through their journey, N.I. became very convinced of the need to encourage and showcase neurodivergent artistic communication, particular in their first love — poetry. Thus, *Barking Sycamores* emerges into the world with a mission: publishing poems by emerging and established neurodivergent writers. We also seek to add positively to the public discussion about neurodivergent realities in the form of essays on neurodivergence and poetics, with special emphasis on neurodivergence's interplay with the creative process. We thank you for joining us on this journey and invite you to read the work in this, our inaugural issue. We will publish new pieces on Tuesdays, Thursdays, and Saturdays until we finish Issue 1.

To George

Sarah   Akin

To begin with,
just a voice —
the tremor
of a chime,
a golden rustle
of half-light,
sustained above
the asphalt night.

Along the streets,
through flowering trees,
so softly
he came to me —
in whispers,
in shivers,
this man
whom I had yet to meet.

And now,
curled about my hand,
tufts
of his fleecy hair.
Skin to morning
skin he is
the sun,
My golden One.

[The imaginary girl]

Emily   Paige   Ballou

was dressed in ruffles and bows,
white pinafores that she didn't ruin,
lacy socks and saddle shoes
that didn't bruise her feet.
She wasn't selfish.
She didn't bicker or whine.
Never talked back,
Knew better than to walk like that.
She did her job
and got good grades.
She set a good example.
She made teachers think good things.
She knew how to say the things
she was expected to say.
Never lied because she couldn't explain.
She was never bitten or kicked,
called witch or fat pig.
Always asked permission
and didn't complain.

[The real girl]

Emily   Paige   Ballou

planned to go away and live
in the woods with owls, deer, and wolves.

So she studied hard.

Learned to blow across the lips
of empty beer bottles to mimic the sound of distant trains,
to hear the prayers of cottonwood trees,
to knead bread dough with small and clumsy hands,
to read the Morse code of fireflies,
and love-songs of robins.

The real girl loved the smell of rain,
of cinnamon, burning leaves, horses, and coming snow.
Chased rabbits through the pine trees.
Dug rocks from a little corner of dirt,
to plant tomatoes, mint, and strawberries.

Locked herself in quiet places and
told no one what she was really up to.

Sang to herself secretly, only while washing dishes.

Stayed awake in bed to hear one radio song
at the same time every night.

Walked through dreams of high bridges over rivers.

Knew that no one was coming.

Could never forget.

The One Who

Amy   Barlow   Liberatore

The one who flinches when touched by surprise
The valedictorian who wore dirty socks to graduation
The quiet boy who stares out the window until
the teacher calls his name three times

The one who deMANDS your attention because
This. Is. Really. Important.

The shy one who doodles in the margins
The kid who screamed during the fire drill, hands over ears

These are people on a special spectrum
A differentiated crystal

They shine differently and in dizzying shades
but shield themselves from
their own beautiful light

An endlessly fascinating array of abilities
Peaks and valleys

Some twirl, some twitch, some
test the water before inching in

Some seem a bit lost

Some see a universe filled with a fierce beauty
that the "normal" could never imagine

Some will not be touched until trust is earned

All shades, all gender identifications, all kinds
All human
All authentic
All autistic

~**Arcane**~

Leila   Fortier

The
Arcane
Colors have
Spilled upon the
Complexity of riddled
Pages where anxious eyes
Are skimming, hungry for relics
Of themselves~ There is a subliminal
Suffering residing within stillness between
The calculation of words and the sweetness of
Breath~ Disguised in subtle gesticulation~ There is
A spontaneous combustion that follows claustrophobia of
The soul~ Elements impossible to neutralize~ Sliding deeper
Into a sea of abstraction if only to elude the absurdity of certitude~
Devouring ringlets of evaporation and making love to the wanton moon

~Lavender Vertigo~

Leila Fortier

*You
Are the equator
Between indulgence and
Abstinence~ Hungry mouthed words
Scavenging scraps of liberation~ Through the
Rubble of past-tenses and perfumed possibilities
The delirium we chase before it becomes ugly
The opiate of experience before twisting
Within excess~ You are the equator between abundance
And absence~ You...the agonizing plenty~ The luxurious
Empty~ You are slow motion syllables sliding over
Contours of blue and untouched worlds
Of fascination~ I am saturated
Within the breath of
Soundlessness
Swallowed
The
Music
Of your silence~
Captured its vibrato within
The temple this body~ This vacant
Body housing far too many irrelevant
Things~ I am on the cusp of crying
Liquid emotions~ Holding fast
Unto its quiver~ Merging
Pleasure with pain-
I know this
Moment
Is as
Fleeting as
It is eternal~ I trapeze
The equator of all your in-betweens
~Both asleep and awake within a lavender vertigo~*

~**Tropics**~

Leila   Fortier

Am

Trying

To   understand

It: These little pockets

Of blue~ The malaise that slips

Between gold dust streams of sun

Like an intersection of interruption~

Were it not for my tropics of elation

Perhaps the unsavory in-betweens

Would take on appearances

Of faint apparitions

Able to be

Snuffed

By

A

(Chamber)

Of

Songs

Where fresh

Blades of grass would

Whisper more important things

About gradients of newborn greens

That dance amongst the dying things

I clutch the invisible worry stone~ Rub

Out the fever of hallucination through

Prayer~ Tethered to the kite-string

Of the next passing ecstasy

In ever reaching

Exaltation

~ ~ ~

~

Everlearner (my mind)

Kimberly   Gerry   Tucker

Everlearner call back
Perpetual Student the last number that called you
too much choice *Scholar*
often equals confusion; wireless everything

Plato Wanna-Be probe the huge arc of the Congo
Curious Cat dromedary manure
(if you want to) *Sly*
is dried and used for fuel

Kurds still fight with Turks oh-*Noble Heart*
amber-rich Belarus *Wisenheimer*
Brainiac still suffers from nuclear
radiation fall-out

retro is in —*Aristotle* and sirocco, chergui and
chili blow in the Sahara ya' know-oh *Socrates*
Pal whaddya' thinka these:
rose oil, hemp, currants, wine and Cádiz?

pineapple *Know-It-All?* shrimp? rice, lumber, tin?
cotton, coal, wool, cattle, palm oil, gems? *Bonafide*
Mensa Member it's an artsy kinda
systematically organized world

use a colored pen *Wise Guy*
to draw a broken line *Einstein* (no-brainer)
and always keep your cherished photos *Everlearner*
in an airtight fireproof container

My Stonehenge

Kimberly   Gerry   Tucker

The tumble of boulders near the shaw
    where He tossed them not too far
    from the highway and billboard ads —
    where rats ran randy
    and woodchucks climbed the whispering sandbank;
I climbed too.

Queen's treasure! Shattered glass,
    scattered by Humankind: gutless teevees
    and ceiling globes —I collected
    shards of sparkling
    brown and green;
dead wine cherished bottle fragments.

Slimsy cloths of faded use,
    where I draped them
    in scant trees
    of withered branches —
    between a rock and a hard place;
My world's curtains.

Chipped mug with Joe's Place logo
    raised dirt-encrusted by My hand
    with upturned pinky finger held so —
    invisible quite real ladies gathered,
    hear My rants; and sip from Their mugs
salvaged handle-less.

At the hollowed out teevee no glass remains
    (they threw it). I rearranged
    it on the sentient flat worn rock
    graffiti'ed cryptically:
    'If You Love It Set It Free;'
there stares the Child Me.

They bask in patchy lot beside the rocks...
    My kitchen nook with makeshift broom
    of string-ed hay and faux stew gathered:
    chipped white wood makes 'chicken,' leaves are 'salad.'
    I sweep the 'marble' ballroom floor —
quaint snakes' boudoir.

Sometimes today the sparsey shaw
    where rabbits hid and once I saw
    a black cat wrestle a snake
    and win —and the sentinel boulders not forsaken
    in their tumble, My Stonehenge; all
appear in My dreams where He put them —

Oriental Horses

Kimberly   Gerry   Tucker

by and large
oriental horses
don't play penny pool but
red-haired villains do —
their King's English

is as you like it
sailors discuss
scuttlebutt
over scrimshaw sessions whilst
lollygagging
longshoremen
comb the Lorelei for ladies
rough and ready
roundheels
stack the deck
burn the midnight oil
but by and large
oriental horses
don't play penny pool

Still Life
Kimberly   Gerry   Tucker

old-world
still life
time-eroded
faded brick
hint of a mansion
never built

old packhorse
dark wet sand
wind and rain
matte black line
moving into the background

end of the trail

entering another world
kinetic individual
lifelike laughter
of the fairies
up on the dark peak

natural rock formations
miscellany of the fascinating
withdrawn
from the tumult of the world
'quite simply different'

"go-it-alone"
take drama to new heights
in broken splendour
shameless coastal castle ruins
still life

Identity Crisis

Jessica Goody

I don't know who I am.
Without a handle to anchor myself,
I am depersonalized, invisible.
I can't stand being nameless, a stray cat.
A name is a title, an identity, but
I am a noun, blank and anonymous.
You asked me what you should call me.

I chose Alice.

Alice tumbled head over heels down the rabbit hole.
I know how she feels. I am in a place where
nothing is familiar, nothing is what it should be.
I can't stand this feeling of floating in space
with nothing to grab on to. It's terrifying.

In the shower, under the womb of water,
I examine myself, taking stock of my body.
I explore it with tentative fingers, drifting
over my scalp like a phrenologist
as if I can feel a persona,
an identity, on the surface of my skin.
There is a scar on my leg. Is it the remnant
of a surgery, an accident?
I read the veins, the freckles,
the wrinkles and scars like Braille.

If my body is a map, a diary of sense memory,
I can retrace my steps. Prick an atlas with a pin,
throw a dart at a map on the wall,
touch a spinning globe with your fingertip.
Wherever it lands, that is home.

Solipsis

Madison Kallisti

Listen: I'm listening. I haven't much time. It's late at night, and squirming out to find you in the little flicks of light between Venetian blinds is blinding. But I'm here. Yes, inside you, squirming to get out. I want to hold you by the sides of the face and turn, slowly, to face what you face. And slump down beside you in the tall grass under the deep starry sky. Yes, there could have been such deep drugs between us, as locked fingers and palms, cold clamp of dirt and hot humid breath between us. But then you would've stood up and said, "Where is the Sun?" And I would have said, "I don't know. Where is it? It's disappeared. And so have we." And you would have been afraid to have disappeared; for how would your family ever see you again? But I would know the rubbing stone between three fingers of safety which speaks silence and solipsis *ad aeternum nobis.* Would've curled up my feet between the brain and rocked myself to sleep in the corner, with just enough light blurred between eyelids to imagine being suckled to sleep in the eye of the jellyfish, the pinnacle of the scorpion, the deep blue sea, the infinitely small cube. Now. What would you call me for falling all the way in? You couldn't know me from outside. But I will swim around you anyway and dream it for you till you see it.

An Abortion, Not Mine

Jillian   Koopman

the small
seed of me
doesn't begin anywhere.
you'd think
surrounded by love—
by nurture
by gray
day, by walls
by shelves by everything really,
defined
that I'd know.
I don't.
oh well.
she once
began with you.
I resent this
monumentally, but still—
the speckled starts
on my part
have also been great;
I have to allow you those.
I don't know why
her face plunges me
why the thought of an
extra limit
inside her body
makes me shudder,
but it does.
it does! I awaken

never ending roots.
oh gorge from which
I emerged, oh lovely
lack I am absent
from, I penetrate
your still wind,
not knowing
where to lay this hunger
that devours me nightly

Seep

Savannah   Logsdon-Breakstone

Even when I
don't like the music
my body seems to find tempo
unless I replace the iron rod
I put there
over years of staring
in mirrors and contorting my face
matching actors and
chiding my voice into
silence unless
it emitted a smooth river.

(endless thoughts
and deeds drowned there-
did I ever tell you?)

as a child my body was

the willow on the banks
bending without resistance
to the currents texture wraught
swirling in eddies of
self soothing green,
grounded little whirlpools
that anchored my sense of self
as I let myself into the music
of every moment.

(later campfires and drums
made do so that the frost
wouldn't make me brittle
enough to break.)

I dug up the
steel posts and pitted
iron years ago but
the rust they left
still leaves soul scars
bleeding from the soil
like some bitter bride's ghost
after her murdering groom
remarries and beds youth
in the bed they called home.

Autocyborgography

Michael   Scott   Monje,   Jr.

I do not exist outside this matrix
of assistive technological accoutrements.
Over-ear headphones double, for me,
as methods of protection
and performance enhancing prostheses,
increasing the speed at which I glean
information from my auditory feed.

I step large through ghost worlds,
using my deus ex apparatus
to influence my peers at a distance,
a digital extension of Hamlet's ghostly visitation.
My legs, too, do not exist as biological implements,
but instead nest themselves in a 2-pedal socket,
converting strides into revolutions per minute.

This new body still proves itself impermanent.
I don't know what I ever expected,
but I am constantly finding this digital existence
is just an amplification chamber
for the same shortcomings
found in my homegrown digits.

Despite the technological enhancement and
exponential growths to comprehension,
the maintenance of my body outpaces
the gains made in my talents.
It's true, I no longer contract the flu,
but a dead battery puts me out a day's work too,

and a bad brake line can do
more damage than a sprained
ankle ever threatened,
not to mention that dementia
is hardly as large a threat to my family
as the theft of my identity
and the subsequent destruction
of my credit by faceless thieves
pulling disembodied heists
across great distances.

Still, when I eschew the tool,
I find my tasks impossible,
for to do-it-myself assumes
that I will eventually settle
for at least a simple set of metal
levers with sharpened ends,
and once I've conceded to that,
the clear line of convenient reasoning
muddies the purity of my vision
and delivers me back into
the grind of machine existence.

The fact is that I am the shape
that the machine has made.
Prometheus was not for us.
His sacrifice brought fire for our ancestors.
The species that needed him preceded me,
and I am the product of its technology.
So spend days staring into your soul,
knowing that the closest to an immaterial
existence humanity has ever glimpsed
is the semblance of your inner self

that bleeds from your fingertips.
Digital existence.
The fulfillment of philosophy's promise
and redeemer of religion's shortcomings,
a physical extension of social construction
finally amplifying not only force,
but the strength of words.

This is my autocyborgography,
the story of how I could only ever be
because of a pre-existing convergence
of a peculiar species of mammal
who was too arrogant
to hold on
to the knowledge
that he was not
of the first people
who knew how to use tools.

Nonouns

Michael Scott Monje, Jr.

That's what they are.
Pronouns are no nouns, they are
instead abstract objectifications:
pointers to the pointers to things.

Meaningless reductions
manipulated by images in the mind
of the speaker,

not in the nature of the referent,
and that's the problem, isn't it?

Being read against preference?
Our corralled existence
is caused by a
meaningless insistence
on protecting
conformity's intransigence.

In stark contrast,
what could exist is bliss.

Sensory-ness.

Cold raindrops quick kiss soft skin.

Friendliness.

Spring things, fling things
overheard in secluded bushes
or beached canoes hidden
among bulrushes.

No nouns in the clean green,
just impressions and recollections
advancing across the surface of ourselves.
All life reduced to verbs,
moving in opposition to
a collective mental abstraction.

A return to real life compels us to keep hidden
all those things that our seclusion summons,
to match performances, and to exist in juxtaposition
to our natural inclinations and normative positions.
It's really time we stopped, isn't it?

Peering Into Infinity

Michael   Scott   Monje,   Jr.

When I'm not speaking,
I feel like two mirrors,
watching myself
watching myself.

Sometimes, I'm
watching myself
watching other people
watch me,
or otherwise corrupting
the perfect fractal
of my own existence
with the disruptive
information injected
by my insistence on observing.

I am Young's experiment,
causing my own collapse by
creating the uncertainty that
I'm remotely observing.

Without an observer,
I am reduced to being
bodies and behaviors;
I build a universe
from ambition:
Challenging myself to
challenge myself and
watching myself
watch myself.

Inertia creeps,
but I already know this.

My couchdwelling
summer afternoon listlessness
is really a kind of quickness,
a key component
to a successful existence.

Just wait and see.

I'll trace futures in wide circles,
draw pictures in the sand,
and make bird noises
until you understand
I'm waiting for *you* to start
keeping pace
with *me*.

1957 (Titicut Blues)

C.F.   Roberts

raymond you've been rotting away in bridgewater state hospital since
                                        before i was born
i'm not sure if they're force feeding you mush in a monkey cell or
if you're finally taking the dirt nap out in the yard
apologies for not keeping up
not sure if anyone thanked you for mom and dad's wedding present
singing castrati in the park trumps waterford crystal any day and
you made the news from whitman to niagra, top of the world, ma
growing up in your shadow was a bitch
afraid of loud noises, not playing well with others
liking monster movies better than football
my guesstimated palmistry led to singing castrati
expectations i caught hints of, expectations i couldn't comprehend
a monkey cell with my name on it
hearing, "he'll never have a normal life,"
hearing, "we have to keep him away from his younger brother,"
hearing, "keep him away from the neighborhood kids,"
hearing, "I had a cousin who was just like you."
your shadow like a millstone, a suffocating blanket
because biology is destiny
because ignorance is morality
because some people can't make the distinction
between autism and violent, homicidal pedophilia
raymond my childhood is locked up with you in bridgewater state hospital
thanks
and on the off chance that you're still above ground
don't bother writing back

At Sixty-Seven, Still Brain Damaged, Still Brilliant

Barbara   Ruth

Words on the stove. Pots in my face.
Swimming in the mainstream, I miss the shark reports.
I miss you like I miss the ends
of all the books I've never read.

My epileptic brain is prone to shatter, spill,
phrases that elude me pool and then congeal up in the ceiling's webs.
Eventually I sweep the shards, ask the spiders to release my missing
        clause.

Tomorrow or the next day I won't be back to normal,
but in the dark
comfort of my inside hands
I feel my mind
shimmering, like rain in a barren land
as alphabets rise up
flash fry in the wok.

Dis/Maze

Barbara Ruth

the labyrinth
refuses still to be your lover.
how can she join you when
you always enter her
with the end
in your sights?

High Summer

Barbara Ruth

Wild cat at my window
sneers at the harpsichorded trills floating from my box;
three part inventions as I
cast about for clothing, checkbook, cell phone, keys.
I need my morning Bach like others need their coffee.
It helps my brain
get organized,
domesticates my mind's essential chaos,
keeps me to my schedule.
"Find me," she growls. "Find me inside of you."
"Cat, cat," I say, "Not now. I'm looking for my medications,
not my inner lynx."
"Wild," she hisses back. "Become the wild.
Where are your savannahs, your rainforests,
where is your watering hole?"

I switch the stereo, slip in a disc I hope she'll like:
calimbas clinking pentatonic gracenotes, but she is not pacified.
Wild cat prefers the rattle and the bass of her own magnetic body.
"High summer," she proclaims.
"Wild summer. Go out into the night. Prowl."

Monday Speaks (For Lea)

Barbara   Ruth

You say I am the day after the sabbath, or the day after the day after the
        shabbat
or the day after the day after the day after
but wait!
I am lunes
luminous liminal lesbianic lyrical
day of moons and so call me as well
moonday Monday marimacha manifestation of miracles and menses
and moving mountains through the meandering mouth of muck
and if you will,
wash your clothes as well.

Poem to Change the World

Barbara   Ruth

This is the poem to change the world.
This is the poem to wrench the war from us.
This is the poem to cancel our carbon footprints.
This is the poem to cleanse the Gulf of Mexico.

This is the poem to ask forgiveness from trees for all my drafts.
This is the poem to redeem myself for all the hours I play
        computer games
instead of working to change the world.
This is the poem to save my soul.

This poem ends genocides
shuts down Guantanamo
satisfies hungry ghosts and lets us all sleep deep.

This poem is the key to the home I'll live in the rest of my life.
This poem is my girlfriend's lucky lottery ticket,
her reward for putting me up and putting up with me.
This poem opens doors and minds through thought control.
This poem stirs your writing, cooks it into a soufflé, a
        Baked Alaska, a manifesto.
This poem proclaims: we are whole, just the way we are,
our wholeness expands holy wholeness everywhere.
This poem seduces lesbians a roomful at a time.
This poem knocks your socks off.

This poem sends the illegal immigrant invaders of Turtle Island
        back to the fifteenth century.
This poem declares all sentient beings citizens of the world.

This poem guarantees safe passage.
This poem is your safe house
your safety net.
This poem is fully accessible.

This poem knows your scars, your scares,
burrows its way beneath your sin.
This poem slips beneath your braces, turns
to ointment for your open sores.
It's a consolation,
              a constellation
              a cancellation of all your debts.
This poem gathers compound interest.

This poem dreams your original face
bears witness to all your struggles, your sorrows,
licks your tears everywhere they fall.

This is the poem for an easy life.
This is the poem you'll remember as you lay dying —
it will sing you through
and the last thought you'll have:
In spite of everything, we changed the world.

A Sleuthian Acrostic

Lucas   Scheelk

Stimming fingers silently orchestrating, while suppressing the
Hums, a piece from an opera he attended at Covent Garden the
Evening prior —his way of

Remembering the music to play on the violin
Later. The overstimulation
Of the senses inspired the creation of his own
Cypher, the stimming fingers, a calming mechanism, the silent
Knowledge of which only Watson witnesses. Decades of suppressed

Hums and buzzes will roar in his bees
Once he leaves for Sussex Downs, away from
London —a London he had just returned to.
Musing on retirement distracts from the
Excitement of persisting crime, for it is
Still 1895.

❖   ❖   ❖

(Camp) Discover(y) – Autistic Community

Lucas   Scheelk

2002

The year I got my first period
The year I attended Camp Discovery for the fifth time
The year my cabin continuously
Sang the soundtrack of The Lion King 2

One week at Camp Discovery
It wasn't enough
One cabin for Autistic girls
The other five cabins for Autistic boys
It wasn't enough

The dial up not reaching
That portion of Lake George, Minnesota
It wasn't enough
Only seeing Autistic adults if they were mentors
          Being Autistic didn't count as having experience in Autism
          To be a camp counselor
It wasn't enough

The caretakers didn't factor
The price we'd pay
For that week in our one cabin
Where we knew that outside those walls
Disabled personhood was neglected

The caretakers didn't factor
That we'd outgrow these
Limits placed against our community

2014

Autistic Community exists beyond the camp
Beyond the Land of 10,000 Lakes

tumblr
dot
com
slash
tagged
slash
actuallyautistic

Dear Allistic,
Love, Autistic

Lucas   Scheelk

(Dedicated to Noel)

Dear Allistic,

I'm glad that you don't wear cologne or perfume. I'm glad that you're not a smoker. I'm glad that your hand lotion doesn't have a strong scent.

Love,
Autistic

Dear Allistic,

Meow.

Meeeow.

Meooow.

Meow!

Love,
Autistic

Dear Allistic,

Thank you for not commenting on my eating habits. Thank you for not commenting on the sounds that I make when I am eating. Thank you for understanding why I don't like to eat around people.

Love,
Autistic

Dear Allistic,

I feel a sense of pride when I remember something you like, or your birthday. It terrifies me that I'll forget everything about you.

Love,
Autistic

Dear Allistic,

It takes me a long time to get used to sleeping in bed with another person. Now that I'm used to sleeping next to you, I don't want to remember what it was like sleeping alone.

Love,
Autistic

Dear Allistic,

After two years, I still hold back some of my more obvious stims from you. After two years, I still apologize to you after infodumping. After two years, I still try to internalize my meltdowns in your presence. After two years, I still try not to shutdown in your presence.

It's not you. Not in the it-is-secretly-you way.

It's definitely, definitely, me.

Love,
Autistic

Dear Allistic,

You've kept the Valentine's Day card I gave you in 2012 in your jacket pocket, which you wear everyday.

You're more romantic than people give you credit for.

Love,
Autistic

Dear Allistic,

Neurotypical people think I'm asexual only because I'm dating you.

Neurotypical people think you're Autistic only because you're dating me.

Neurotypical people are fucking weird.

Love,
Autistic

Dear Allistic,

We share a dislike of lettuce and olives. How often we go out on dates depends on time, location, noise level, and mental energy. We both like cats; for me, at least, that's an understatement. You like milk chocolates. I like 100% cocoa dark chocolates.

You find your heroes in The Avengers. I find mine in Sherlock Holmes. You don't drink alcohol. I drink seldom, for a multitude of reasons. You go light on the caffeine. I need multiple daily doses of caffeine. I do not share your value of sleep.

"Boyfriend" is a term of endearment we both share.

You give meticulous detail in the costumes and wigs you create. I do the same in my poems.

Love,
Autistic

Dear Allistic,

I hope to always find new ways to write about how much you mean to me.

Love,
Autistic

Path of Emergence

A.D.   Stone

The eyes of the Moon
solemnly shine,
a tender gaze upon the heart of Night.
Freezing feet crackle,
cloaked in solitude upon a frigid path;
unfurling alabaster shimmers,
beauty longing to release its majesty.

Hidden fractals cry out:
Sun, comfort these fragile bones,
give strength to delicate feet.
They wait to manifest a glorious uprising
at the first sight of Dawn:
buds bursting tiny joys of luster.

As brisk winds stroke frozen cheeks,
Fibonaccian perfections
unleash spectral streams —

an ever-lasting unfolding canvas

for those with spirits determined to seek

the magical in the midst of Shadows.

Holding My Breath

Angela Weddle

I imagine you precariously poised on the diving board. Your entire life has been a leap of faith. This time is no different, as you jump, jump, and twirl, less like a sea creature, more like a bird, with legs spread as wings into the water. Twirl. Splash! Splasssshhhh! Ahhhhh.

Your technique was a bit off. But high scores for whimsy. The water rushes into you, as red plumes gush out. You are still innocent, though.

I haven't met you, yet. I am practicing holding my breath —a useful skill to have, I would later learn. I am not balanced enough to take leaps of faith. My faith comes in incremental gulps and exhalations, my rib cage about to burst with hope and sadness. This may not seem an impressive feat, but I am the one who cannot breathe, the girl with the pink snorkel (I wanted blue).

I wanted to go deep. I love to go deep. The way I would one day go deep inside of you. Taking you in, feeling your coral reef, swaying, peeping in and out of your crevices, tangled in seaweed, ecstatic, rising to the surface, like a beached whale, moaning, and your tides pulling me in, never letting me go back to the land. I would gulp and easily hold my breath for you, so that you could take the leap. But you know nothing of this, yet.

See, this is our love story.

I have never been good at holding my breath. All of my thoughts and feelings rush to the surface, coming up from the deep. They have restricted me to the shallow water and given me this dammed flotation device. I am out here with the children, bubbles coming from their noses. And the instructor tells me that my kick is crazy. My chest expands. And all of these sensations threaten to crack me open like the crab legs I had for dinner.

You will later tell me that I am tough. But I am a soft shell crab. Always molting. I know good places to hide. You will perfect your technique in the intervening years till we meet. You will learn to dive with your legs closed.

I have been coming up for air for so many years: the pressure of the water against my rib cage, the lightheadedness, and my vision fuzzy. But I am persistent, my kick still wild. I have learned to float on my back. I am such a hard worker. So much effort goes into my kick. And so, my technique is a bit off, too. But high scores for effort. I have learned to propel myself around the pool, with great speed. Spasmatic thrusts, gulp, and the real secret is timing. No one tells you that, of course.

There are others who can hold it longer, who have better form. But I have developed my own rhythm. Thrusting and bobbing, gulp, ahhh, huh... there I go, cheeks puffed out, chest at full capacity, and I am going in. Going deep. Never content to stay at the surface of this pool, of my mind, of these feelings. Of you. Of this love. Our love. But you know nothing of this, yet.

Coming up, kick, kick, arms flailing. I do not glide through your moist terrain as an angelfish, might. I get caught in the pitted surfaces. Tangled in you, wrapped in algae. I come up to the surface. And the old reality is gone. I check to see if you are real. I feel smooth flesh, and you are radiant, your skin the color of the most delicate shells. You are not flying any longer. But floating. A mermaid. I have been practicing holding my breath. But you know nothing of this. This is our love story.

I am no longer a crab, though I still think like one, sometimes. I want to crawl into your crevices. Hide and then seek. We are as children. Your leaps, my gulps, Splash! Ahhh!

I, too, have a tail. I look at the hard shells protecting my breasts. I have been practicing holding my breath. I have been taking incremental gulps and exhalations. To you. My technique is a bit off. But high scores for effort. I am on the diving board. You are my leap of faith. I have been practicing hold my breath. This is our love story. Here goes...

Clear as Damon

Christopher   Wood-Robbins

The rules are clear
as damontage
of pick out on left
fielding questions of
what an autistic person goes
thru the wood-be sting
operation of meet
the pressing issues of
what does it menial
the time and spaced
out the door to the judges
chamber music of lies
and blackmail call of the wild
jungle tree-swallowed
by a sharp-toothed
allegation in court
of law and ordered chaos.

Globe of Scarlet

Christopher   Wood-Robbins

for my wonderful wife Julie Simoes

We float through air
on a globe of scarlet
and sunshine yellow
far above and away from a world
that has no time or inclination
for us.
We sail over the uncertain fields
of pine trees below us
before we rise above the clouds
and suddenly try to grow accustomed
to a surprise burst of intense sunlight,
then we look down
on a bright wonderous landscape
of glowing pearly clouds
and imagine ourselves as horses
galloping on a celestial riding range.
Our love carries us away
from chaos and uncertainty
and into the joy
we sought for all our lives.
This is all we need.

The Resulting Light

Christopher   Wood-Robbins

In outer space, a battle unfurled.
Hostile factions from different worlds
fired off lasers in a desperate race
to claim the riches of this quadrant in space.
Two of the warships veered off course.
In a tragic display of misguided force
and blazing fury, they collided head on.
In a terrible soundless roar, they were gone.
As if to salvage this unfortunate plight
for a greater good, the resulting light
crawled its way down through the filtering sky
of a virgin blue-green planet close by
where three good kings of reverent mind
took the light for a "star" and exclaimed, "It's a sign
that bears good news for women and men!
We must travel at once to Bethlehem!".

Ellie   Castellanos

UNTITLED

Kimberly Gerry Tucker

FAUX VAN GOGH

Kimberly Gerry Tucker

ORDINARY SPACE

N.I. Nicholson

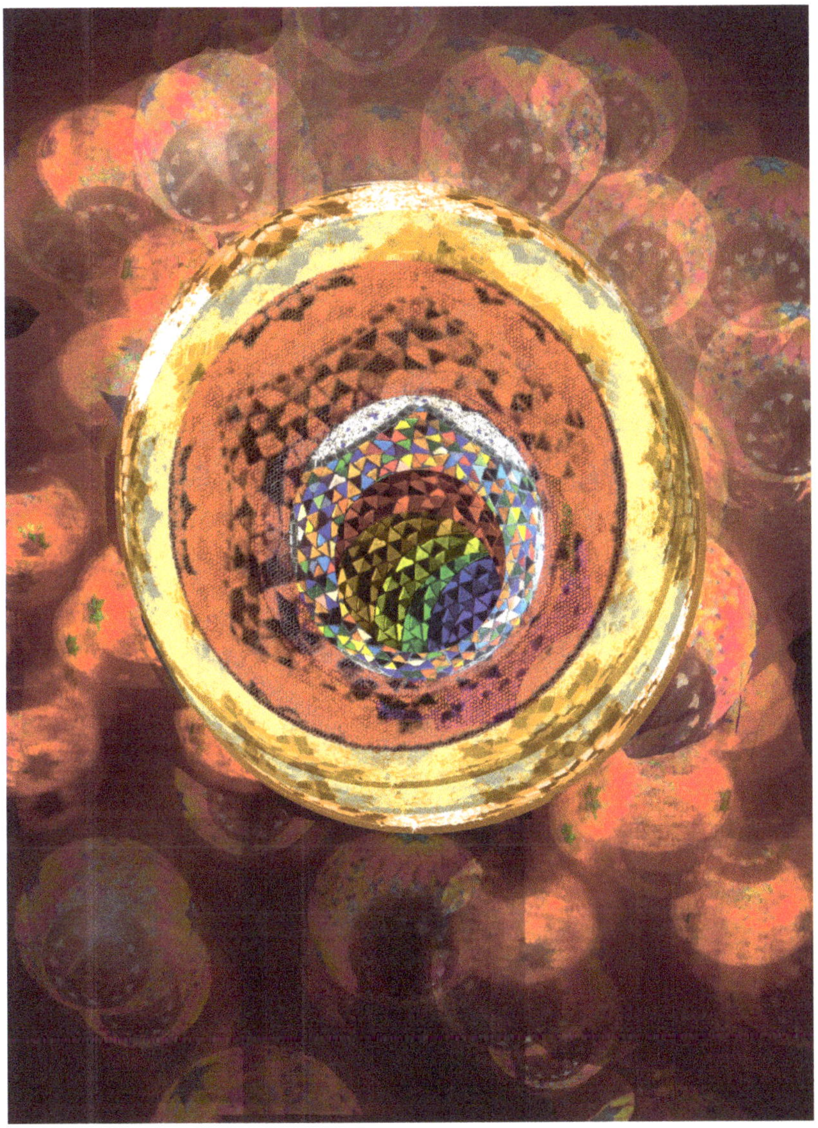

I AM VIBRATING AT THE SPEED OF LIGHT

Candy Waters

SELF PORTRAIT

BARKING SYCAMORES

Issue 2

Summer/Fall 2014

Issue 2: Summer/Fall 2014

(Cover Art: N.I. Nicholson)

Introduction: Issue 2
If Thine Eye Be Single

Welcome to the second issue of *Barking Sycamores*. We praise and thank The Divine that we've been given another opportunity to present a variety of neurodivergent poetic and artistic voices. We also thank our Issue 1 authors and artists for taking a "leap of faith" with us and making Issue 1 a success.

Selecting work for a themed issue proved to be a bit more difficult. However, we chose to approach our theme, "If Thine Eye Be Single", very broadly — and we encouraged those submitting work to do this as well.

As some of our readers may be aware, our theme for this issue comes from the Bible — Matthew 6:22-23 (King James Version), to be exact. The original verses appear as part of Jesus' Sermon on the Mount:

"The light of the body is the eye: if therefore thine eye be single, thy whole body shall be full of light. But if thine eye be evil, thy whole body shall be full of darkness. If therefore the light that is in thee be darkness, how great is that darkness!"

When we thought of those words, we immediately saw some neurodivergent themes emerging — namely, single-mindedness and hyperfocus. For example, the behavior of autistics who seek to intensely know a subject or interest has been called "narrow, obsessive interests" by others. While this tendency has been sometimes portrayed in a decidedly negative light, we tend to think of it in more positive aspects. For example, N.I. proposed in a recent blog post on *Woman With Asperger's* that autistics may use these interests to better understand the world around them. And in an article published in Shift Journal, Julie Bascom of *Just Stimming* spoke of the joy she experiences when engaged in her interests:

"...the experience is so *rich*. It's textured, vibrant, and layered. It exudes joy. It is a hug machine for my brain. It makes my heart pump faster and my mouth twitch back into a smile every few minutes. I feel like I'm sparkling. Every inch of me is totally engaged in and powered up by the obsession. Things are clear."

Also, we've witnessed neurodivergent folk of all stripes demonstrate intense hyperfocus on tasks or hobbies for hours. We consider such behaviors as potential strengths with positive outcomes, not weaknesses or pathological behaviors to be discouraged. These characteristics encourage a deep understanding and attention to detail which enhance the quality of not only the person's interaction with the subject or task, but any resulting products of it.

We also thought about themes which speak to our common humanity — namely love, devotion, and vision. No matter what type of human we are, we have the capacity to experience these in our lives. And when we speak of vision, just as Jesus can be interpreted to not be literally speaking of the eye in those verses, we also do not necessarily mean vision in a literal manner but in a broader sense of taking in observations, impressions, data, and information.

The theme also reminded us that we need to continue tossing aside limiting ideas created by organized religion and those co-opting Jesus' message to support *status quo*. Jesus himself challenged the *status quo* on many occasions by promoting social justice, by calling for compassion for those maligned in first century Judean society — women, the poor, and others not favored by the religious elite of the day, by questioning the idea of ritual for its own sake, by encouraging us to love both neighbor and enemy, and by suggesting that we radically change our thinking in terms of who we consider to *be* our neighbor.

It is this message of social justice promoted by Jesus — and others considered to be enlightened humans throughout history — with which we align ourselves. Social justice means many things — but in this particular case, it means promoting acceptance of neurodiversity and ending prejudice, discrimination, and harmful practices towards neurodivergent folk. Similar to Captain Jean-Luc Picard of *Star Trek: The Next Generation* who proclaimed in the first episode of that series, "If we're going to be damned, let's be damned for what we actually are", we present Issue 2 in all of its glory and color, beauty and strangeness, with no apologies, and with eternal thanks to our poets and artists in this issue.

Doodles

Cathy   Carlisi

As if Klee or Picasso were a spider,
there's a web of daisies and fish,
cupcakes and bubbles—marginalia
that never fails to include her name
with a heart as the dot on the "i."
Her teacher shakes his finger:
"Your art is grand, but you need to pay
attention."   To pay is to exchange
something for something else. Trade
the mind's wanderlust for 5th grade
algebra. It seems harsh, like military duty
for a toddler, asking an infant to read
Proust. So we give her our good paper
and pens, point out swirls and swoops
at the edge of her pages, often forgetting
to mention the numbers that add up
to so little.

Quicksand Devotion

Tasha Chemel

Wracked by prayer, shaking with psalms,
this is all I am: devotion.

The urge to submit strikes whenever it pleases.
I am at the mercy of unplanned devotion.

I befriended a couple Greek goddesses, but it didn't last.
I balked when they demanded devotion.

I am bored by stained glass, bored by steeples,
bored to tears by others' bland devotion.

I worship golden calves, just for the hell of it.
Nothing is more stunning than banned devotion.

I write stacks of letters to lost lovers
attempting to resurrect our sham devotion.

Find me a rescuer, or a remedy,
lest I succumb to quicksand devotion.

~Parallel and Proximity~

Leila   Fortier

I had to stop reading~ Stop between paragraphs, sentences...sometimes the words~ So enthralled...so inebriated~ Terrified of some inevitable end...between the chase and pace of it~ Lost within the infinite of possibility~ A thousand translations, perhaps~ Paused within invocations of blue~ Conjured by words~ A drink, a meal, an interlude~ Eros, absence, and vista~ Unified unto the experience~ Transcending the moment into a blinding glare of white light~ No word, no metaphor...no page to be forgotten~ Clung to as close as breast is to self...incapable of separation~ Returning always to nurse of itself~ As if the nearness of ink to page; proximity of page to skin, and skin to bone would never...ever...be close enough~

Why am I weeping? In the throes of abstraction I touched upon forbidden truths... and perhaps those truths pain me~ I am a poet unworthy of such a name~ I call upon you: My untitled poem of mystery; of revelation...of absolute...of nothing~ Yet...here you are: My everything...my concrete...my tangible nonsense...my lie~ I adore you as pulse and blood; as tourniquet and noose~ My newborn...my deathbed~ My fragments of resurrection~

Wide-eyed and bewildered~ Starry eyed in any-case~ Agony and passion... unspeakable~ Nothing will ever suffice the intent of this expression~ I slay myself as unworthy sacrifice~ In the splendor and elation of morning sun...my blood of golden ambrosia~ To be so worthy as insignificant in this great process~ My true love...my absolution and envy~ My painstaking thrust into the deep unknown...finding bitter-sweet refuge within parallel losses of sanity~

~With me...of me...and still nowhere to be found~

~Sensory~

Leila   Fortier

Isn't it enough
To be caught in
The crossfire of
My   longing?
Feeding   my
Hunger   within
A cage of
Resistance~
Sexless   aching
At the juncture
Of untouched skin~
Your eyes have
Become foreign
To me~ Yet the
Words   within
These   silences
Always   make
Their   way home~
I arch again to
The splendor of
Tide~ Braced
Against   the
Backside of
The moon~
This place
Barren of
Bodies~
Tracing
Formless
Ecstasies~
Toward   the
Knotted coil of
Untouched bliss~
Untangling in its
Waking~ Tendrils
And   tentacles
Of sensory~
Arising from
Its sacred
Wor(l)d

Introduction to "The Outlets"

Kimberly Gerry Tucker

Carry around a magnifying glass all day and aim it at everything and nothing in particular. (No focus.) But what happens when it's placed directly in the path of hot sunlight and purposefully aimed at dry leaves: they catch fire.

"If you chase two rabbits you will not catch either one."
— Gary Keller, author.

Slow down, Kim. Try not to be so scattered, I would tell myself. In the writing of my 2012 book *Under The Banana Moon*, I purposefully focused my lens; or my "turning point," into creation.

It is true, writers can't NOT write. Curse? No, rather a blessing.

Turning points have always been channeled into the creation of art and written works. Diaries and journaling are suppositories for emotional constipation! (I kept 17 of them growing up.) When my husband got a terminal illness in 1999, the timing was bad. But then there is never a correct time to hear someone has 5 years to live. My middle son was suffering with his own medical issues when we got the news about his father. My oldest son, a teenager, was battling anger, angst and apathy. My daughter, at 5, seemed too young, carefree and delighted with life to be burdened by crisis.

Crisis spares no one.

Eventually tears, shock, sadness, helplessness, and anger morphed into faith, patience, hope, acceptance and humor. But that was a slow percolation. Writing was a necessary ingredient in this process.

The following poem, "The Outlets," was written in the early stages of his illness (Lou Gehrig's Disease; or ALS). I was hyper-aware of the people around me who were suffering. This poem is about:

I. my older son, newly diagnosed with ASD, was immersed in a gnarly twilight zone between teen years and adulthood. He was hurting for his father and dealing with puberty too; as a person on the autistic spectrum. He cut himself a lot as an outlet for everything difficult inside him. We "got specialized help" for him. He's a college graduate now and has a loving family. His scarred arms do computer savvy things and hold his daughters with care. He's a FAR cry from the mixed up man-child that used to open gashes in his arms.

II. my middle son became uncharacteristically aggressive. His features were plumper; his expressions angrier, as a result of the steroids he was taking for his 20 hour sleeping spells, asthma attacks and the welt-like rash that would appear all over him out of nowhere. He was missing school a lot and the meds were changing his gentle spirit. He did heal, over time. He is now the gentle spirit in the family; a real wit like his siblings, and a wonderful and patient father.

III. "the young retired roofer", my husband, whose ALS wasted his muscles.

IV. me, I lost a lot of weight — 85 pounds give or take. As caregiver, I was using the feeding tube, yangour wand (phlegm sucker), and breathing machine correctly (surprising myself, harshest critic) but I was doing so much that my identity fell off. It really did. It was as if it took a Lemming Leap. The person in its place was often told: "You look like hell." To which I'd reply, "I'm getting it all done."

V. and finally Les — a friend of a friend who continued to create art (painting on tins) throughout his lung cancer ordeal, an activity which sustained him mentally and financially. He was full steam ahead — living, creating, with an eye on the present.

My sweet five year old is briefly mentioned in III. J.J. of this poem. She would go on to write an amazingly insightful chronicle of this crisis period in our lives. Everyone has stress. Everyone deals with stress and unplanned crises so differently. I wrote words in neat lines on a too-bright unreliable dinosaur of a desktop PC, sometimes at two in the morning. (It still had floppy disk capability, if that puts it in perspective.) The writing was my axis. In fact the book I mentioned earlier came of this writing period. The writing was interspersed with studies of Buddhism, the strengthening of the third eye. Writing lined things up neatly. It put my proverbial ducks in a row. It wasn't a panacea, and in fact "The Outlets" isn't even a great poem as far as poems go. (Editors' Note: we beg to differ about the quality of this poem.)

"The Outlets" serves as a mile marker on an unplanned journey that others shared. It was an intentionally aimed magnifying glass onto the computer page. The written words were the fire. The act of creating taught me that time, perseverance, patience and faith were the things that could extinguish its flame.

The Outlets

Kimberly   Gerry   Tucker

I. J.M.

The blackened room's his cage.
Its young dweller, a serious lad —
is prone to fiery flares of rage.
He selects a shard
of glass, maybe —or a pin or knife
to add
a long red scratch atop the scars.
Release.
Down falls the guard.

II. J.J.

Consumed by bouts
of anxiety, sickness and dread...
the husky boy slouches home.
His once gentle spirit has bled
out. So he's prone
to eruptive squalls from mood changing
Steroid pills that fight his illness
and change his will.
He shoves his whiny sister, so cruel!
Even gentle teasing sparks a rage —
a punch to her arm until she cries again...
A bully, you!? His mother fills
a tepid flow and assures her son
this time his eyes won't scare away
the sandman, but sleep is nothing

more than blood returning full force —
what is she healthy for?

III. H.R.T.

Wasn't that you under the blazing eye of so
many summers? (Now gone by.) Swinging
hammers held so high? Nails-in-mouth,
sun-kissed muscles that would never fade?
Weren't you the one whose muscles fed, clothed, and
sheltered the lot of us? And bade...
me hello and soon goodbye of the permanent kind?
The one who never drifted off to bars after work but poured
himself home instead? NOW
as pounds disappear from your solid frame
I thought I saw you again in the screensaver of the
flickering mouse potato screen- our home pc
but it can't be, you're a new man.
Can it be? HOW? The neuromuscular disease is not a dream?
My kitchen window oversees
the yard, the one you cannot mow —and Fuque
it all-somehow you are
larger NOW than before. On the canvas I beseech
my hands to capture your chi.

IV. ME

The quiet organizer frump, genteel, well-read,
long labored to shed
the weight that had bare-knuckle held
after three babies; life was plump,
never bland. Enter crises. Guilt.
Quicksand. Do you get the gist?

Well she built a cyst around fond collections
and mosaiced broken pieces onto sections of
everything.
Her identity is flying, crying.
Her psyche's laid bare. As she
walks a narrow line —losing half her body weight
and hair and not even trying.

V. LES

In a city built into the north, Britts live;
Les with cancer, painting flying tea kettles.
The lungs are dying, the hands are flying.
Monetary and therapeutic rewards come of this —
he paints and sells his old tobacco tins.

My Body

Jessica   Goody

For me June is the cruelest month.
All summer, actually, May through
mid-October. As the humidity swells
my body responds with tension.

It flowers
and threads its way through my stomach.
Every flash of lightning psychically
electrocutes me. I feel the ripple effect
in every joint and vein.

It is like a contraction, a seizure.
I cannot control my body.
The sudden stiffness sears my muscles.
My stomach tightens in fear.
I cannot breathe.

Anticipation of summer storms
occupies my thoughts. I am consumed.
I desperately try to distract my thoughts
from the irrationality of panic.

After the storm cell passes,
I tentatively venture out,
nosing cautiously as a Londoner
exiting the Underground following an air raid,
picking through the rubble
of fallen stone and broken brick.

Panic Attack in Neo-Natal ICU

Jessica   Goody

This is where it begins:
can you imagine lying
in a glass coffin, like Snow White
strung with tubes and wires
like tin-can telephones or
strings of Chinese firecrackers,
tucked into conduits and tethers?

I am only earthbound

by the sterile rubber, the plastic, the glass
hoses linking me to my cell like a pet, leashed and caged.
Some tubes fat as tunnels, others noodle-thin.
intravenous, oxygen, shunt, catheter,
lung-pumper, pacemaker.

Can you imagine
an extended sense of awareness,
the way a cat's whiskers tingle
and his fur rises
when it's about to rain?
Prone, supine, straining.
It must be how Helen Keller felt,
black blindness, all-encompassing.

The beeping
of monitors, thermometers, air-tubes;
the hiss of artificial breath, raspy and stale.
Every bodily function
measured and rated
until you become your own timer, a human clock,
regulated and regular, nervous and precise.

Senses

Jessica   Goody

My hands are old before their time.
They resemble a sage's fingers, gnarled and ancient.
My sunken joints and wrinkled knuckles possess an odd elegance.
Flickering tendons meet the green cobwebs of my veins,
my fingertips provoking the rhythmic chatter of the keys.

My hand flops flounder-like
at the end of a narrow wrist,
hanging limply, curving
in the spastic arc of the lame,
its bitten nails like broken seashells.

The twitch and ticks of sudden spasm
belie the fierce concentration required
to cross treacherous parking lots,
avoiding cold puddles and broken concrete,
loose steps and stairs without railings,
divining the clearest route across a room,
sensing the texture of grass underfoot,
divots hidden amongst the green.

My thick, heavy foot and flailing synapses
rely on my sense of touch
in order to make my way in the world,
stumbling between crowds and along rough terrain,
seeking handholds for security,
testing the air the way a snake does, sightlessly,
with a flicker of its tongue, scenting shapes
and objects unseen in the dark.

The Mermaid

Jessica   Goody

"We have lingered in the chambers of the sea
By sea-girls wreathed with seaweed red and brown
Till human voices wake us, and we drown."
—T.S. Eliot, "The Love Song of J. Alfred Prufrock"

I.

The mermaid wears a mask.
Tubes drift from her nostrils,
linking her to an oxygen machine,
missile-shaped and metallic.
Her tail hangs limply, dangling from
the wheelchair seat.

Out of water, she cannot walk, cannot stand.
The air she breathes is blue and cool. She cannot adjust
to the smog ashore.
Scales wink and gleam on her hips, her fins,
like a starlet's evening gown.

The surgery separating her webbed fingers went well.
Tiny purple scars line each digit. Her fingernails are
nacreous, like mother of pearl.
They scraped the barnacles from her shoulder blades,
surgeons in white deftly wielding gleaming scalpels.
Round, puckered scars remain, in the same spot
where, earlier that morning,

an angel had her wings removed.

Fluid drips wetly into her nasal passages
from the boxy plastic shell of the nebulizer.
She relies on artificial air, asthmatic.
They have stitched her gills shut,
the angled slashes of scars pitting her abdomen.
She craves salt. The doctors warn her about cholesterol
and sodium, unaware that her kidneys,
used to filtering seawater, are unaffected by salt.

Pulled from the water, her color has faded.
They want to surgically remove her tail. They plan
to outfit her with prosthetic legs. They demonstrate
with models, cheerfully flexing kneecaps
false as doll parts.
The prosthetics are pale and statuesque,
machine-made. Knee and ankle joints are bolted,
plastic and hollow as a mannequin.

Cutting away green sequin-scales,
they insert a metal rod into her hip.
They are trying to carve away her aqueous identity
and replace it with that of a tin man, a robot.
Scars crisscross her ankles, her insteps.
They will fade, eventually, to the color
of a crab carapace, abandoned and bleached by the sun.

You have to stare to see the hidden scars,
the ones on her scalp beneath her Technicolor hair,
the ones from when they drained her brain,
swollen with seawater.
Her hair will grow back, curling and colorful

as flower petals. Green, lapis blue with red streaks;
orange as a tiger lily,
dashed with gold glitter,
mica, stardust, grains of sand.

They have scanned her, X-rayed, MRI'd.
Her silhouette glows from radiation.
Her heart appeared onscreen, red and stuttering,
a chambered Nautilus.
They have performed every test, gluing wires
to her chest, her tail, her skull
to see what a mermaid's brain looks like.
Her metabolism is much faster than theirs,
her heartbeat, cold-blooded, much slower.

Dry and removed from the succoring ocean,
her skin is dull and roughened. Her scales
are sloughing off, and losing their gleam.
The orthopedist traces her bone scan
with his finger as he talks:

Her hips are narrow,
her tail, where he legs should be,
tapers to the points of her diaphanous fins.
Her knees are twisted, wanting to kiss each other
instead of facing forward. Her joints push and tug
toward one another in a scissors gait.

Dragging along the dun-colored corridor,
she is floppy, uncoordinated.
They tell her to build up her muscles.
Draped in the shapeless hospital gown,
her previously tangled hair clipped and shorn,

She cannot make them understand:
her body was not made for life on land.

II.

They fill her with electricity,
with distilled stars.
The names of the pills are elaborate,
like the Latin names of seashells:
Thorazine, Lithium, Stelazine, Sertraline.
She frequently feels heavy, leaden,
or like she is floating. It is not a kind sensation.
She is unwilling to be swept out to their
psychopharmalogical sea. She wants to go home.

"You do not come from the sea," the psychiatrists say.
They attempt to hypnotize the truth out of her,
to smear it from her mind, the way the sea smooths
away words scratched into damp sand.
She will not tell them her secrets:
the songs of the whales,
the Morse Code of echolocation,
the silent wisdoms of moon and sea.

"Delusional," they say. "Psychotic features
represented by hallucinations. She believes she is
a mermaid, a mythological creature."
According to their files, the manila folders
of endless prescriptions and transcripts
of talk-therapy sessions, she does not exist.
According to them, she is an impossibility,
a figment, a persona from folklore and fairy tales.

But she must be real, they have seen her,
touched her. Their hands, their machines, have
examined, tested, probed. They have collected her blood,
her urine, her pulse, weight, and temperature.
How long will they keep her here?
She is drifting like the seasons.
Away from the sea, she cannot hear its call.
She can see the topaz eye of the moon
from her steel-reinforced, unbreakable window
in the psych ward.

You

Elizabeth J. (Ibby) Grace

"If thine eye be single," she said
And I knew it was holy; yet holy mackerel
You know what I'm like: I laughed
And could not stop. My mind made
The green guy from Monsters the movie
With the M on his hat and so then,
Of course, my mind made you
Making me laugh some more.

You are the one beyond imagining,
Even though my mind makes kaleidoscopes
And waterfalls, and dreams of helix
Soundscapes of refracting light I can fly on,
Shimmering dapples dance color and float
In ways I can't even sing so much less say,
And I live in a great haze of spacey joy sometimes:

None of that compares
To the beauty, the paradise you are.

But it is holy. The Greek word, here "single,"
Is haplous, which usually means 'simple.'
And the rest of the verse has your body full
Of light. So I am simple, and blessed. I thought
I would be alone, and this was fine with me,
Because I had not met you yet then.
Now that I know you, I will never be
Without you, and this is why
My mind makes you hear what I hear,
See what I notice, knowing
Your magical laughter will move my merriment

Forevermore.

[There's a chicken!]

Duane L. Herrmann

The phrase my son and I
say with glee to each other
when our conversation
jumps several tracks:
"There's a chicken!"
and we laugh knowing
that our brains
do not in straight lines go
but whirl in circles
and spirals with tendrils.

"There's a chicken!"
And we howl.
It's so nice to know
we're not alone
or mentally deficient:
We Have Chickens!
And they fly
as they will.

Addiction of Poetry

Thomas   Krampf

Stripped of
its delicate boat-like
blossoms

The poppy prepares
to drop the dark opiate
of its seed

To satisfy the cravings
of the earth —

Benign Positional Vertigo

Thomas Krampf

My shadow is suffering from vertigo

It cannot stand up, sit down, turn around,
without the risk of falling over

"Maybe it's a defect in some inherited composition of
the brain," I say, "After all, the reality is while the earth is constantly
rotating, we're also orbiting at great speed around the sun.

"You mean there's some temporary impairment in a corrective
mechanism of the brain," my shadow says

"I wonder if anybody else ever thought of that?"

"I don't know," I say, as in the oscillating light,
and afraid of the import of my own words,
I grip the edge of the table.

A cow at 18,000 miles an hour whips past the window.

Burning Tobacco, or Reflections on a Suicide

Thomas Krampf

This scavenger hunt
this mess, this chaos, in my studio
this is what it is

Krampf's Special
My Grandfather was a cigar maker
I open a small wooden box
with its fragile hinges

I am shocked. Inside
I find my Uncle Norbert's cigarette case.
I had forgot how I inherited it
or even who gave it to me.

He died.
I lived.

To a faint odor, I snap open the prematurely
elegant silver lid.

Like a tribal elder, in this exotic but tender
offering to the Gods

I am holding the continuation of his life
in my hands.

The Book Mark
Thomas   Krampf

Opening my notebook
and as I carry the concealed
weapon of the word

I hear the sibilant hiss of
the snake skin

And know yesterday, like a book mark,
where I left off

And where tomorrow, a dangerous
frontier, I must enter

but stepping carefully —

The Migration
Thomas   Krampf

In my genealogy
I am a child born
of a migration

and thrown into the sea

And like Jonah
in the belly of the whale
to be regurgitated, time

and time again

on the shores of a Promised Land —

Conditions of Victory

Michael Scott Monje, Jr.

We have within ourselves the ability
to trigger the cultural singularity,
to break the rate of change in society
and create an ever-shifting reality
wherein consensus exists by degree.

We already have access to the past's playthings.
Anything recorded after the thirties,
or shown on TV after nineteen sixty,
is still mixing in the gestalt of our identity,
influencing our descendants,
and obliterating the generational rule of three.

The technology for preserving history
has invaded the haze of sacred time
and relegated the bulk of our species' written existence
to a kind of single-media dark age
that only serves to buttress us against prehistory.
The books are dead, long live the booklings!

The cyborgs might try for parity,
but even if they succeed with their singularity

I have to think that we already have them beat,
because with the mythic's existence crowded in with
actual records of historical significance,
we can bend ourselves into the shapes of our wishes.

Here is what I already see:

Racism we thought was left in the fifties
perpetrated by craftsmen with handlebar mustaches
who insist they are not pirates,
nor are they trying to bring back
the fashion of the eighteen nineties.
This is mixing in with a conspicuous consumption
of the previous generation's bewildered teenage
ramblings, causing a traffic jam
of appropriated angst
among well-fed flower children
who do not realize the radical nature of their
common kindness,
because their own contextual blindness
obscures the relatively recent addition of twee
to the rest of our cultural vocabulary.
Riding between these living
examples of our cultural timelessness,
are the gray ones, and the remembrance
of their technological achievements
are affectations the young pick up.
They are selling their past
to insure their retirements.

I think we can go further than this.
The rate of change I see is accelerated,
and no doubt the cyborgs have helped

by giving us the means to communicate
much more quickly than we ever anticipated,
but our self-congratulation should be
deferred until we at least agree
upon our conditions of victory.

Here is the vision that comes to me:

Acoustic raves programming DJs to remix Bob Dylan
as Amish youth on Rumspringe cop green corn,
sucking lungfuls to fuel their attempts at a cabbage patch
while their sisters rock traditional bonnets full of Molly,
swaying in the breeze of finger-picked dubstep blues revival melodies.

Someone has fifty-fiftied Skrillex
and Stevie Ray
on two turntables
and set them to competing.

Instead of this, kids who know the impermanence of society
are using it to take advantage of me.
Even as they pet laptop screens and order robots to do their laundry,
they are using these tools with the mockery of tourists,
showing my hope for the future to be just another fucking commodity.
The truth is, for all my blog updates and lightspeed communicating,
I'd rather be on the front porch refinishing fine furniture.

I straddle the divide between the indulgence of present desires and
traditional understanding, demanding someone see
that change is not worth fighting, but that it comes with the cost
of retaining and understanding other contexts,
lest the souls of all the artifacts
used to build your social existence

be lost to the remix.

Hip hop taught me this—the recycling of history in context,
that sampling need not be appropriating
unless it's done incorrectly.
It can instead be transmitted history.
The enjoyment of new creativity
is simultaneously
a reflection on past experience
and a building activity.

I dream of days where I walk barefoot across the rolling hills of others'
        creative landscapes,
and oil paintings I can't recognize spring up in my footsteps.

I remember Salvador Dali, but his discipline is not for me,
I will not stop at dripping clocks or subsume my sexuality publicly.
I have no taste for sham marriages, less for restraint,
and nothing but contempt for the anonymity of masked orgies.
The twentieth century can keep these,
along with Gatsby, comedy roasts, Geddy Lee, and Emily Post.

I will be taking de stijl, abstract expressionism,
absurdist theater, the Beats, all the music,
my university degree, the words of Aldous Huxley,
and the hopes of a generation of flower children, now grown,
who see themselves as primitives with smartphones.

But my neglect of that other subset of artifacts
does not change the fact that they are still part of my habitat.
This is why it's called a singularity—
culturally, we are on the verge of accommodating all things.
Can you see yourself tipping over this edge,

beating authoritative voices back with their own artifacts,
and indulging in a riot of ideas?
Or do you fear the chaos?
Are you El Salvador de los Dadas?
Or just another narcissist waiting to play boss?

Anyway, Ray Kurzweil can curse us while we
take his toys away and refuse to let him play boss.
By the time his robots overtake us, I plan to have
a cultural landscape that accommodates them,
and maybe then the cyborgographers can see
that we were never opposed to their way of being.
We just don't want to keep being overwritten;
the reason we breathe is to carry on tradition.

AA/BB/CC

Barbara   Ruth

A fundamental pause.
A searching for the cause.
A chance inanity
Then quick calamity.
So goes it, so it goes,
Where it lands, everyone knows.
Contrails in the sky
Gouging out the eye.

A Brief Natural History of What the Wind Blew in Motel

Barbara   Ruth

If only the wind only blew things into me.
If only there only was one wind.

I never say "the wind." I never call myself a motel.
Somewhere in the sixties someone started that name as a joke,
a defamation, some say, and I was one, but now I think it started out as
        nautical hijinks,
Some California Coasters, looking out to sea from the bar at
        Dew Drop Inn,
Procol Harum on the jukebox, with a God's eye hanging underneath
        the mirrorball;
One head turns to another and says, "Whatever happened to those
        sixteen vestal virgins?"
And another, seeing me on the horizon replies, "That's them now,
        at What the Wind Blew In Motel."

They've been here, both the hippies and the Vestals, baroque in their
        G String Bach
debating exactly where is the epicenter
the cyclone's eye, here in this constabulary.
Some made it to the coast of Madagascar, caught
the Chinooks in Alberta, bumped into Raymond Chandler with a
        Santa Ana migraine,
on the lookout for wildfires and docile eyes (those eyes get dangerous
        when plural)
turned murder, gritting, "Anything
can happen." Miss North Dakota bragged, "My state's the Saudi Arabia
        of wind power,"

but wait 'til Greenland brews up a contestant for Miss Universe. Wait
        until you see Miss Mars.

So many shades. Forty eight passengers and five crewmembers from the
        Andrea Doria.
I keep a room for Van Gogh, silent, dark, for when the Mistrals release
        him from his easel in the maize.
La Llorena, weeping for her equine lover, lost in the Horse Latitudes
        when becalmed sailors
crazed by doldrums, made killing choices to conserve their larders.
        Now we only eat
our memories. And search the iris for the I of it.

The winds blow in because the only way to bear
the Williwaws, the Foen, the Pitaraq, the Bergwinds, the Oroshis,
        the Dust Devils,
all the rest: open all the windows, doors. Let it all come through.
This is the true eye, the I and I, the eiderdown
you wrap around your sockets.

I call myself An On and Off-Shore Inn With Attitude
but you'll most likely knows me as What the Wind Blew In Motel.
At your service.

Hg
Barbara   Ruth

Each day I would watch it July in my hair I was seven I stood on the
fried grass while the wind
whipped the sheets dry somebody must

have told me to come in
side but I stayed
stared at the needle the surge past 115
120 not a careful child but patient certain something would change me burn the world
pure I glanced up to the caw
crow wings sparkling like coal on its way to diamond I turned back to the wall
now splotchy with afterimage rubbed
my eyes clear
in time
for the burst, the shatter
glass up
up through the bulb and I
caught it a shape-changing ball no thought just offered
my palms to receive sacrament from the temple of no
return. Quicksilver writhed all over my life
lines, my love lines, my Mounds of Venus, and I did
what I've done ever since when tracking the unalloyed light and suddenly
Body of God erupts finds its way into my hands
I
stroked it, forsaking the face of my fathers, I
swallowed
it
down.

Sampling

Barbara   Ruth

just a pre-
agrarian diet
try it
for a fortnight
bill of rights
knights
in white satin. vote
no on all bespoke
overcoats.

two, three, many Vietnams
the Holy Land
language of fans
you don't need to be a weatherman
to pick up the gun
a few words written in the mothertongue
a day late. freaked out. abortion
was our Vietnam. it's my lot in life
Lot's wife
turned to salt
be thankful for what you've got.

March went out like a lion
but she doesn't have a lot to say.
coldest winter was the summer i spent in San Francisco
open your golden gates
betcha can't eat just one.

lullabies from the axis of evil

suicide in self-defense.

it's been swell having lunch with you
feather boas
Frank Boaz
hanging chads
that went by fast.

Thief of Souls

Barbara   Ruth

It started the first time
shudder shutter   shutter shudder
the first time a man
if they find you they take you
a man stared and pointed
snap! shutterbug   shutterbugs
pointed it at a child
shutterbugs scout and swarm
directed, "Now hold it!"
shutterbugs snatch
dictated, "Now smile!"
if they find you they take you
sh! sh! shutterbugs.......
and squeezed.

Domestic Abuse

Jonathan Travelstead

What Failure eats, *you* eat.
Pushes it on a tray through the slot in your office door.
Failure lifts your tongue, shines a light
so he sees the milky thinness which clots your throat.
Knows what you left unswallowed, unfinished.

Fact: Abuse is more sustaining than gruel

No one's seen you in weeks.
The screen door whinges open and you hear a knock
but he answers. Muffled voices. *Sorry. Haven't seen him.*
Then they're gone and light slashes your face,
pricks your irises closed when he speaks to you through the chain
They're not your friends, they just want something.

You're fine with it.
You need rules tattooed into you.
When you're uppity, and when you talk back.
Slap! Three scarlet lines on your face,
a staff for the hand's blunt palm it transcribes notes upon.

Because you did it wrong.
Because you're *Telling* instead of *Asking*,
and because no one gave you any fucking permission.

Fact: A domestic case attempts leaving six times
before succeeding, or dying, sometimes both

What you believe: Better the devil you know

than the one you don't

You are Failure's bitch.
He makes you cry but still you let him fuck you
because you believe this is how he shows love, because
you forget what *let* means, and because just maybe
if you keep your head down long enough
you will finally earn it.

————————————————

You say at first he only watched
when you gagged your first breath in this world
After: Surveillance you say
he's been conducting your whole life,

studying your hungers and habits
he holds first up to Watson, then Skinner,
as if examining them against light. He knows you
and the latest self-help books by heart.

Has filled a legal pad with symptoms —yours —
he apes for shrinks he has beers with
Tuesdays at the Corner Tavern. You say
he works for Blackwater,

but cannot say anymore on that. Right.
You say he gives you a foot less than the line
you'd need to be found necktied
to a lead pipe. He's published papers

on interrogation. Improved the effectiveness
of water-boarding and the verity of truth received.

But here you are, talking to me,
unafraid even if he is listening. Grimace,

and your exposed cuspids send my mind
trawling its own watery past until it makes
a harbor of depression. Just who are you?
Wink your red, bloodshot eye, and my breaths

half their depth. My anxious mind considers
the infinite micro actions between the pleather seat
and the fire door that must be taken to exit.
I don't want any trouble,

I've borrowed enough. You say
One of us is a liar, divide, and the new guy
who sits in the other seat points,
Don't believe him.

———————————

Blame the furies you divide your natures into for how your life
saws in always one of two directions. Blame the sociopath glassed on pills,

The Mothman, or a cryptid not found in the genus of *homo.*
One gibbous moon, and you split like a quince. Halves fall, and a lycanthrope's

anatomy is exposed. Canine kidney beside your fur-sprouted spleen.
Pin the blood you found greased on the brass doorknob to his hirsute ass,

and feel the tip of a lawn dart piercing your own. Culpability.
Take the orange pill and give Big Pharma credit for the column of checks

beside the maintenance sheets for your truck, motorbike.
Your color-coded spreadsheets, alphabetized and dated. Take nothing,

and spend the day watching a made-for-tv Mr. Hyde bludgeon your character
with laziness' ballpeen. You're the archetypal drill sergeant

who trafficks in fungible time, measuring progress against a ticking clock.
Stay out late and rubberstamp yourself deficient. Ground-pound

an extra mile as punishment. Say it wrong, hit the books.
Truth is, haters gonna hate, but every day, it's the same with you.

Hand to lying mouth, then mouth to fool mind. Alibis. Eye witness sketch
of a baddie everyone knows is you but you swear's just an aspect.

A man, divided, stitched together. Man with one face that's handsome
if only because it's defined by the boils on the other. Man,

you really have it in for yourself. Dualities you separate,
and try herding back in the private room, thinking they should do anything

other than fight like children, or cats with their tails tied.
Every fireman needs an arsonist. Winnow all the dark out of the night

and something in the lighthouse is gonna break.

———————————

Sometimes your life is a house which burns even in its foundation, only
the flame's in the walls and rafters in a wavelength of light you can't see
With the naked eye. No warning system chirps *lo batt*, or *Alarm.* No sirens,
No lights warbling over the scorched, hanging soffits. No neighbors
Gathered outside the property's perimeter shout *Jonathan! Come out!*

They don't have the proper instruments for detecting heat in the void
Spaces. A thermal imager's LCD indicates rising temperature
By white on black, and you're just a ghost smudged between
Washout and jet, floating inside a lukewarm sensory
Deprivation chamber like a frog in a warming pot.
If you weren't counting piggies, but stood
Instead outside in the weed-cracked street,
Would you see what curls from you,
Shimmery with heat, and lapping
the night's star-black?

———————————

Make a coat of your apprehensions
You slip into. Big spoon to your little spoon,
Insulated this way in worry,
Dream of eighteen. Clad in spandex,
you straddle a bicycle's frame across Iowa.
Subsist on wind, movement,
and chocolate milk.

Let go your self-stung
Flesh and float above so you see its repose.
Times there were other motivations.
Times now you could walk out
On this volatile sack of chemicals.
Get a job at a diner. Make tips.
Cycle around the lake.

Outside of yourself, you see
Your apneic tensions also snatch and grab
for breath. Your parts share orbit,
Sprout from a single hub.

Calm desire. Stay your palm
from the red button
which jettisons your shame.

No more violence, no more
separating your humors from the good guys,
dreaming a razor across the street
of the bad one's arms,
then down failure's river.
Extinguish self-loathing,
and dish out only wet coals.

Return, but wake slowly
Accepting what comes in the susurrus
between low ebbs. Make love over
your mortal wounds.
See how borders overlap,
how, a larger sum
than your smallest parts,

You suffer together a little death.

Pleasure Principle (Pitbull Pills)

Jonathan   Travelstead

Eight-fifteen. Still in bed, I crunch the capsule, grind the orange
spheres between my teeth, bitter as early walnut. In the gym,
discipline's steel shank grows in my bones' calyx until they split.

Fluorescents thrum like light sabers. Radiant as the drug's pathway

from sublingual muscle to reptilian brain to fluttering chest, *om* —
the Vedic's single vowel, resonates outward through pectoralis,

pronator teres, my fingers. I'm coming up beneath a loaded flat bar
which bends my torso forward, the exercise called a 'Good morning'.
Five sets. I snatch-and-clean until my hams, glutes, and quads

are depleted uranium, napalm jelly quivering in the place of legs.
If anyone else is here I don't see them, jaws locked and tightening,
present only in this moment's flagellation. No clanging of dropped

plates or discordant, heavy metal from the gym's speakers. Only
hum. The pitbull sergeant's glottal *UP! DOWN!* How long have I
been here? Skull crushers. Upright, two hands pincer the dumbbell,

extend it above until my triceps have the quality of shredded meat.
My shoulders tighten in the focus the bench press demands. Unrack,
lower, then piston up, blood rushing like hydraulic fluid to where

it is needed. I am the servant, not the master. The engine, but not
the engineer. It feels like sex, the *pump. DOWN! UP!* Until you're
sure you'll rupture a muscle like an overinflated tire, radial blowout

so the steel belt shows. Trembling with exhaustion you cannot feel,
you only know failure by the curtains descending over your vision
when someone appears, helps you guide it to the hooks. Beguiled,

tachycardic and puking, you lust after this pyramid built by slaves
in a top-down construction. Failure. Recover. Drop weight. Again.

Symbiosis

Jonathan Travelstead

Failure yanks the logging chain his pet slipped around his
own neck, mashes his nose in it. *This is what he wants, and this is
how I'll give it to him.* And so the pet welcomes this hard knock motivation
handed down like a knot at the end of a string of generations

that skipped his Father the Giant with his callus-armored hands,
soft speech, but which he doubles down on himself. He doesn't say anything when
Failure tears pages from Pumping Iron magazine —
Boris Vallejo prints from movie posters and covers for dimestore

Fantasy & Erotica. He licks Failure's feet when he magnetizes the
wrinkled, ragged-edged pictures in a mural bordering a round spot
in the fridge's stainless, mirror finish so when he goes for milk
he sees himself surrounded by all that he isn't.

In one, a string-clad bimbo —Sappho, or Eros —clings to Conan
the Barbarian's leaden calf. Single arm upraised, he stares at his own
acrylic bulge of vein thundering over his bicep and broadsword.
Beside it, another Boris in caricature of the first

on a National Lampoon's poster. Subjects: An adoring Beverly D'Angelo
at the knee of a hypertrophic Chevy Chase, complete with
shit-eating grin, and mugging the camera as he thrusts a tennis racket
up to the storm of sky. Conan, or Clark Griswold,

each is a reminder for how he falls short of self-portraiture,
and so he uses Failure like a two-edged sword, choosing the belief
that he's the diva worshipping at cock-level of the playboy
who only kicks sand in her face, guffaws her mosquito tits and lumpy butt,

her capellini triceps' atonal definition. He forgets about plateau,
how gains cease when the muscle is worked the same way every time,
and now Failure thinks he's been calling the shots so long,
he's not going to give up control so easily. Soon,

laughing like a loon imitating a hyena, he jerks the logging chain
too tight to slip off, and this time when he smears your face in it
you come away with a bloody nose. You start believing when he says
your voice is too tinny and shrill for barking orders, or even

to make the tryouts for "America's Got Talent". Now you know
there's no such thing as a fifty-fifty relationship, only temporary mutual
benefit until someone commits a coup. You used him,
now he gets to use you. He's the one with the scissors. He's got the glue.

New Messengers

Christopher   Wood-Robbins

(a dedication to open mic artists who dare to question the status quo)

Zany
Yeomen w/
X-ray
Wisdom
Vow to
Unravel
Tight-kept
Secrets
Regarding

Quacks in
Power, and
Outraged
New
Messengers
Lend the
Key to
Jesters
Investigating
Hypocritical
Gods to
Find out that
Elitism is
Deemed
Certified
Baloney
After all.

The Printed Page

Christopher   Wood-Robbins

I am
The Teacher and the Learner,
The one who strives against a world
Of computerization, bureaucracy,
Exploitation and bigotry
For these are the forces that rob our dreams.
Today, many are in danger
From Old Men to New Women,
From Nordic Gods and sullen ships

To Civil Rights Marchers and Harlequin Lips.
A single ignorant flame
Can wipe out a multitude of worlds
And leave a poor excuse, an electric winter
Harvesting the corpse of humanity
Unless we fight the technical cage
And defend our right to the Printed Page.

N.I. Nicholson

LET THIS BE MY LAST BATTLEFIELD

Miss Roberts

HEAD (SELF-PORTRAIT)

Maranda Russell

DEEP SPACE ABSTRACT

Candy Waters

RADIANCE

SUNFETTI

Issue 3: Fall/Winter 2014

(Cover Art: Samm Almester)

Introduction: Issue 3

We began publishing this journal on April 1, with a lot of support from various groups and folks: the first poets and artists appearing in Issues 1 and 2, the NeuroQueer community on Facebook, the Awe of Autism, and many others. Our little journal was tweeted about and shared. And we are proud of our first two issues.

This summer, we began reaching out to creative writing programs across the United States and asked them to share our call for submissions. We also began to accept short fiction for our journal. The response was enormous, and we had the difficult task of choosing poems and short fiction for Issue 3.

This third issue is like a musical piece in many movements, an amalgamation of many aspects of the human experience sung from a choir of neurodivergent literary voices. We feel it is decidedly a bit darker in tone than the first two issues. Ice formed in our bones after reading some of the works, and other works extracted shouts and tears from us. You could say it was like ascending a mountain, and we quote from "Bright Lights" by Gary Clark, Jr. to sum up our experience: "I went up a different person, came down somebody else".

We invite you to read and enjoy Issue 3, including its cover art by digital artist Samm Almester. A hearty thanks to our writers, readers, and to those who shared us all over the internet. You're helping us grow, and we are indebted to you as we journey further into the undiscovered country: our future.

At the Lake
Matthew   Brown

for my dad, Lawrence H. Brown

You summed it up —North Wisconsin, Granddad's cottage:
Proselytize it piece by piece from cabin to bourgeois house.

(Logs hide in plywood; fieldstones give way to granite.)

Your wish: to cover my knotholes and black holes.
Your words: "I honestly don't understand how your
Mind works." My hand rearranged corn kernels
The ground squirrel would eat.

(Lake-facing porch pulled down, paneled living room,
Color television and carpet added.)

You worried because I said things to people
Like, "Why does your car make sounds when
You slow down?" Whispered my own private stories;
Shook my hands in the air before me;

Missed the goings-on because I was outside
Looking at trees, or downstairs listening to records
That might be evil: the Beatles, the Doors.

(Drop ceiling covers rough-hewn rafters.)

And yet, you did everything for me.
Once you stopped so I could pick up a piece of wood
From the cutting of a favorite oak by the courthouse.

You put miles on the car and paid good money
To help me. Concessions were made at college
So I could drop math and add literature.

(At least the new kitchen and bathroom looked right, built
Of half-logs and knotty pine, hammered hinges and
Strap latches.)

As time went on, you mellowed and spoke no more angry words,
Loved your grandchildren with a great expansive heart,

Regretted you hadn't done more to help me
Find something gainful to do with my writing.

❖   ❖   ❖

They Taught Us

Tasha   Chemel

They taught us to be curious.
If we couldn't find curiosity, they taught us to be good actors.

They taught us about power and privilege
But we still cowered when our male professor spoke.

They taught us to measure our empathy in a steel beaker.
Saving the surplus for our supervisor's scrutiny.

They taught us that our clients had the right not to answer
But in supervision, our silence was defiance.

They taught us theories and their theorists:
Minuchin and White, structural and narrative.

They taught us to analyze and hypothesize.
They did not teach us humility.

They taught us to diagnose and assess
To derive freedom from putting people in boxes.

They taught us to distinguish between content and process:
How not to fall for our clients' obfuscations.

They taught us how to interrupt and redirect
But firmly and sweetly, to soften the sting.

They taught us about trauma and repetition
To fear stagnancy and revile obsession.

They taught us that if we read bits of our past
on our clients' lined faces

We were the ones
who needed therapy.

Walls

Deanna   Christian

Commercial mower,
Mangled doe
Dying horribly in tall grass,

Spotted red...and spotted white?
Two fawns, unafraid of their mother's killer.

They struggle to stand
On the slick shelter floor,
Calm in strange surroundings.
Not frightened by the curious teenagers.

Only one thing surprises them: the walls.

Walls surprise me, too.

❖   ❖   ❖

Night Logger

Allen Davis

Colorado sat atop the armored personnel carrier and stared into the darkness. The tanks and PCs were arranged in a circle, wagon train style. Beside each was a sandbag bunker. Encircling everything was the concertina wire — big, high rolls of barbed wire. In the event Charlie was able to get close, claymore mines had been set up in front of the vehicles facing the perimeter. Except for one guard on each track, everyone was asleep.

He picked up the starlight scope and slowly scanned the area in front of him through the faint green glow, left to right, right to left. Occasionally he stopped at random to examine a certain spot. Nothing — no movement, no suspicious shapes. Every scan looked exactly like the previous one. Exhausted from a long day in the heat following night after night of not enough sleep, he struggled to keep his eyes open. He took a swig of water from his canteen and rubbed his eyes — still not able to shake the heavy tiredness. He would have slapped himself but didn't want to draw special attention from Charlie.

A voice jumped out of the radio, startling him. "Echo Three. What is your sitrep? Over." Though relatively low in volume, it sounded impatient, as if it had been calling him for a while. *Shit!* He had fallen asleep! He recognized the voice as belonging to Jefferson, a black guy on the command tank. Although he had been busted down to private E-1, he knew his shit. Colorado quickly called in a negative sitrep to give the impression he had been awake the whole time, but Jefferson wasn't fooled.

"Listen up!" he said, the anger showing through with the volume barely increasing. "You're not Back In The World anymore!" And he proceeded to ream his ass up and down and inside out. Colorado was embarrassed and scared — not of Jefferson, who he liked and normally got along with just fine — but of what could have happened. Plenty of guys had fallen asleep on guard duty before and so had Jefferson, but that didn't make it alright. Camps had been overrun before — GIs killed in their sleep — so there was simply no excuse.

Resolving to stay sharp, Colorado slowly scanned his section of the perimeter again with the starlight scope. Then he put the scope down, looked left and right into the blackness and listened carefully, trying to put his entire body in tune with the night. When he looked toward the right again, something felt ever so slightly different. He couldn't decide what it was. Movement? He didn't think so. A different shade of darkness as his eyes adjusted? Maybe. Or perhaps the temperature had dropped half a degree and he had sensed the change without registering it. He wondered if he had nodded off for another second but didn't believe he had. He picked up the starlight scope once more, pointed it to the right and held it. Seconds crawled by, minutes. And then he saw it — or thought he did: a dark green shadow near the ground shifted right and stopped. Was it Charlie? A small animal? His imagination? He kept the scope trained on that spot and held his breath so it wouldn't shake. The shadow moved again! And again! His pulse quickened and his hand trembled as he grabbed the handset.

"Echo Three to Echo One, over."

Thank God Jefferson answered right away. "Echo One to Echo Three, over."

"I have movement. Request permission to fire, over."

Before Jefferson spoke there was a heavy pause. Colorado could hear him thinking: IF CHARLIE FUCKS US UP IT'S YOUR FAULT!

"Echo One to Echo Three. Permission granted, over."

Colorado eased the safety off of the fifty caliber machine gun mounted on top of the PC. The fifty weighed more than eighty pounds and was so powerful that previous models had been used against tanks and airplanes. He held the dual handles tightly, pointed the long barrel low to the ground and fired. *Boom! Boom! Boom! Boom! Boom!* His fire was quickly returned with the menacing *crack-crack-crack* of the AK-47. From the circular formation other fifties boomed; M-60 machine guns rattled out long bursts, red tracers zipping into the night. M-16s popped, a claymore blew and flares whooshed up into the sky like Fourth of July fireworks. *Doop!* went an M-79 grenade launcher, followed by an explosion. As quickly as it had begun, everything stopped. Smoke and the smell of gunpowder lingered in the air.

As soon as it was light enough, Colorado, Jefferson and a few others went out to investigate. Between Colorado's sector and the one on the right, just inside the concertina wire, lay a barefoot body dressed in dark clothing. It was face down and looked like it was sleeping. When Colorado got closer, however, he could see numerous dark splotches of blood on the shirt and pants. A few feet away lay a bloody shoe. A hole had been cut through the bottom of the concertina wire.

"That's *your* gook, Colorado," declared Jefferson. "That's *your* gook."

Jefferson put his boot under one of the shoulders and turned the body over. The front of the shirt was covered in blood. Most shocking, however, was the face. Smooth and boyish, it had only a few smears of blood and dirt on the cheeks and forehead. The dead man looked about sixteen or seventeen —just a couple of years younger than Colorado — and reminded him of the good natured Vietnamese kid who lugged cases of beer at the enlisted men's club on the base camp every morning. He leaned a little closer. It was him! The kid opened his big, playful, dark eyes, jumped up and started laughing hysterically, his musical, high pitched giggles skittering through the air.

"Fool ya!" he chanted. "Fool ya! Fool ya!"

He tore open his bloody shirt to reveal nothing underneath but a bony brown chest and sunken stomach.

"Cut!" yelled the director.

Evening Play

Melissa DeHart

"Darling, why don't you come inside for a bit? It looks as if it's about to rain!"

From where she was on the swing set, Jenna heard her mother call to her. It was indeed getting cloudy, which made it easier for her to see Charlie, and although she was sad to go inside she knew her friend would be there. She jumped off her swing and pranced across the yard, her golden hair bouncing about her oval features. Mother stood just inside the door, her apron covered in flour as she was in the middle of making supper.

"Is supper ready?" Jenna asked, her brimming blue eyes looking up to her mother.

"Quite nearly, dear," was the response, and the little girl grinned in elation. "Why don't you go play with your dolls for a bit while I finish up? Be careful not to get anything on your white stockings. I don't want you ruining another pair."

"Yes, Mommy!" Jenna cried as she ran up the stairs to her play room. Bounding into the first room on the left, she was immediately surrounded by porcelain dolls and various wooden doll houses that her father had built over the years.

"Here, Charlie," Jenna said, gathering the most comfortable sitting pillows in the room and arranging them in the center as a sort of impromptu couch. "You can sit on these while I play. Do you want a book?" She paused, earnestly reading the empty space before her. After a moment she hurried to the far wall where a low bookshelf stood, loaded with her favorite stories her parents had read to her. She studied the worn spines for a moment before pulling out a copy of Alice in Wonderland. "I know it's a girl story," she explained, moving back to the pillows and setting the novel in the center of the pile, "but I think you'll like it."

Jenna went on to play with her dolls, generally berating her stuffed rabbit for being unruly. The smell of her mother's cooking slowly filled the room while the clouds simultaneously darkened her surroundings. Jenna did not move to turn on any lights, but instead smiled as it grew darker. Finally, just as it grew into a gloomy dusk the little girl glanced over at the pillows and smiled. Stretching out from the spot was the antithesis of a shadow — a glow of light cast on the floor in the shape of a small boy, its figure stretching to the far wall.

"There you are, Charlie!" Jenna cried in happiness. "I was hoping you would come out today!" No voice answered her as she watched the shadow remain still. Her mother, had she entered, would have said that the shadow was merely that of the doll sitting on the windowsill, but Jenna knew better. As she played the shadow became lighter, much to the contradiction of the darkened state of the room. Minutes passed and not only did the shadow become lighter, but light itself, an untethered lantern upon the cushions.

Jenna looked up and smiled at the sight of her offered book being picked up by a sunbeam hand.

Qreaux

fayola

my words and thoughts aren't horizontal like stripes.
i am as many water drops as will
fit on a penny before it bursts.
my clique types, critiques, speaks, freaks.
my clique just is, too.

we, like i, is not necessarily one,
but we are more united.
i always knew [but didn't own that]
i am
as i am
just as i bring
the unique critique of the
ableist obsolete.
the movement is identity and security
of our own FREE ISH.
we say many things.
listen.

❖   ❖   ❖

Neurodivergency

Jessica   Goody

"At last, I began to consider my mind's disorder a sacred thing."
—Arthur Rimbaud

I survived the Holocaust of birth,
the poison palace of the womb.
One quadrant of my brain is blank,
oxygen lost like air from a broken balloon.
In my mind's eye, that hollow is dark,
a clotted cave of scar tissue. Elsewhere,
brain pathways are lit like switchboards,
thoughts blinking like turn signals.
You can see the nerve-socket glow,
trace its trail from synapse to cell.

The ego delights in taxonomy, sorting the population

into neat categories: "normal", "perfect", "strange".
Imaginary words, transient and impossible
as the ever-shifting horizon.
All neurodivergency is the same.
The tic and twitch of Parkinson's Disease
isn't all that different from the spastic's spasm:
The complicated electrical mechanisms of the mind
are controlled by the same mental motherboard.

The brain rattles in a dance of the ancient trickster god.
Numbers and letters flicker on the page like butterflies
defying capture, evading lepidopterous nets and corkboards.
Perhaps the silence of the autistic, the selective mute
is a defense mechanism against society's noise,
the volatile verbosity of Tourette's Syndrome
a simple refusal to let his subconscious go unheard.

Arrival

Laura   Merleau

If I'd never loved
Within the domain of
The real numbers
My heart would never
Have known you
You of the left and
Right, up and down,
Backward and for-
Ward —you of
The irresistible, blissful,

And intoxicating

Binary —all those
Who enter this realm
Exist within an axiom
Of choice reaching
Heights of emotion
Impossible for the
Humdrum world of
Ordinary action —still

Flying into heaven,
I'm coming to the
River, the ocean,
A mathematics accepting
The promise of each
Heart remembering
Who it is by
Remembering who

It loves by loving
Who craves the
Consequences of your
Transparent philosophy

Being Nobody Special for You

Laura Merleau

The door of my tent
Has opened onto a new
Forest —a forest too
Beautiful for me to
Understand, and with
One foot on the wing
Of a bird big enough
To fly me to the water-
Fall at the edge of
Knowledge, I lift off
Into an evolution

That is quite different
From the one I'd grown
Accustomed to the
First half of my life

While the second half
Of my life has this
Inescapable instinct
To fly everywhere on
The wing of a nuclear
Bird in the helium
Core of a sun becoming
Not hotter or colder
But just right as your
Entire dynasty becomes
Mine in the blink
Of my third eye which

Had been closed so
Long but now is open

Wide to let in all
Our race is destined
To turn into with dignity
With detachment and
Plenty of letting go

Contributing to Neuroscience through a Wish

Laura　Merleau

I looked at my watch.
It was time. The sun
Met the different planes
Of physical and astral
At just the right angle
Yet pulsed at variable

Frequencies. Forgiveness.
It would increase para-
Sympathetic activity and
Thus produce relaxation
Followed by a profound
Sense of peace. So
How to get there from

Here. I sat in my tent

Listening to a strange
Source consisting of
Scintillating radio
Signals. The day was
Fine, and there were
No birds singing for
The distant call of
A voice from somewhere
Unseen. In the sun

And hotter stars, I
Hoped to find a prayer,
A sense that my wish
Was becoming physio-
Logically real. Hope
Consisting of rapidly
Fluctuating intensities
Of bright prayers for
Forgiveness came slowly

Across the distant
Emotional abyss, filling
The gap where before
There had been only
Neurological puzzles.

Impersonating the Bird in Your Heart

Laura   Merleau

If you are not who you
Seem to be —who are
You? Are you a figurate
Series whose one-dimensional
Terms are the natural numbers?

Are you a broken wing
Vanishing in the forest of
Diagonal terms from left to right

Upward? These facts could
Render the determination of
Your stellar age much simpler
Than could be imagined,
Wondering why X keeps expanding

While your heart goes on beating
At the same steady rate,
Y = 64, which does not
Equal more than it did
Yesterday. So the numbers
Are a relevant digression, yielding
A Thank You-You're Welcome from
No beginning or end in

Sight. Maybe a big
Please will appear later.

Maybe the rows of the Pascal

Triangle will demonstrate your
Name in rows of a practical
Theorem here and now where
The wing is going to heal.

You Know Hope When You See It

Laura   Merleau

In the short period of half
A life span, you proved
Your existence theorem

No one-way journey but
Branching out like a table
Of logarithms and their
Corresponding antilogarithms

A breakthrough in chaos
For a theoretical physicist
Who studies the sun's
Energy field merging with
Her own to make one

Energy field —making
Use of the rule of the
Logistic Equation, cascades
Of lifetimes doubling —
Splitting   the wealth

Of energy that comes

Pouring out into numbers

Then you are back here
In your body, bending
Your right leg and stretching
The left one sideways
Stretching over to touch
Your right hand to your
Left toe without pain

For a concrete representation
Of something better than
Before when suffering
And pain occupied more
Time than any search

For truth, though there is
No vague doctrine involved

There is only a whole new
World out there —yours
For the breathing in

Condo Steps Crawl

David   Mitchell

Remember when you said
You called the police
For our daughter's own good?
She was crawling on the stairs

For Christ's sake!
She was out of her wheelchair
Unaccompanied
A disabled minor
A girl without a chaperone
A kid without an adult
A daughter without a parent
She could have scraped a knee
Or stuck her head through the railing
Broken the decorative Hosta
And I said, But call the police?
Isn't that a bit much?
What were you reporting?
A disabled person loose in the world?
An abandoned wheelchair?
A disabled girl making a way
In a house with stairs
An alley too narrow
And filled with gravel for looks
A ramp too steep to navigate by herself
A lift that took three people to operate
That's a world where there is no way —
When the cops showed up
They waved their guns
Acting like they were on
The easiest bust of the day
So overreaction was appropriate
Cause we were the only ones endangered
The ones they were there to save
The ones they were there to charge
The ones they were there to lecture
Don't let this girl crawl up the stairs
Parental neglect, child abandonment

Making her make a way out of no way
Did you know that it is a crime
To be a disabled person out in the world?
That calling the police creates a crime?
There are all kinds of coming outs
And all crimes if you call attention to them?
And you said, Just a neighborly thing to do.

Moonchild

Thomas Park

I started on a poem, "Knocking in Hells Door" about re/rocking a soul that had been compressed, grinded and cutup for consumption by an insatiable world. It was on a back page. It's about how the world sniffs us up her nose, sweats us out her armpits, or blows us out as boogars if we let it. It is about reoccurring visions/death.

It's bad when we do not recognize that people are sick, and sometimes the funny behavior we whip our cameras out capture is a gesture for help... Umph, a naked young man at the bus stop on Peterboro at 2am. Umph, Umph, a old black woman with no legs getting pushed down the street by a man with one leg in a shopping cart.

I keep me wondering when my blue skies will stay, and life will give us butterflies instead of pain. I don't care if people don't like me anymore. It takes to much energy. It's easier to try to love everyone through my binoculars. I need help most days. I am poor. I am rich...I am enough.

I am behind I will never finish my work; neither will some of my dear readers...so sad about Michael Jackson, and Robin Williams, and Whitney Houston. So happy......we are breathing. A little black genius has been born; the savior from Al-Masih ad-Dajjal, the evil one.

In Islamic eschatology he appears pretending to be the Messiah at a time in the future. Ya Allah! I seek Your protection from the torture of hell, and Your protection from the torture of worms scorpions that sting me in the grave. I have not been to the mosque in a solid year. It's a long way away. I am an Island.

I am ashamed island. I went to a church ten or fifteen times, it is Orthodox. A great man lectures there. I have written poems about the mosque, poems about the church, and a hundred poems underwriting madness and butchering classic to post contemporary depression.

If I had a group; aspirants wouldn't be hazed, need a tattoo, or have to come from the right side of the tracks. I would like people to stay balanced. I wish I could share my schedule, no time for a nap. I am listening to guys talking about the late Heavy D...looking at a video of Hendrix practicing in London.

Some kids just rode past sitting in the back of a loud, white, dented and scratched, eighty-five, Chevy farm truck. They were smiling, hollering, and shooting super soakers. They were from the trailer park. They were so happy they can ride fast on the back of a truck speeding down the road.

It's bad when we do not recognize that people are sick, and sometimes the funny behavior we whip our cameras out capture is a gesture for help... Umph, a naked young black man at the bus stop on Peterboro at 2am. Umph, Umph, a old black woman with no legs getting pushed down Harper in a shopping cart by a man with one leg (smoke) the grown man in the motel-stiff Batman Costume, minus tights trotting down Harper in the middle of the day; ashy legs and all.

Playing the Waiting Game

Thomas   Park

I linger for him
like lilies under the sun
coping, hoping that he will come
nearer to me. I missed him last night
and the night before. Sunday week
we were together he and I
a Grand Marnier, and Ben Webster
he and I white sheets and a new pad
in the middle of the master bed
we were one, he smelled like coconuts
he said I smelled like teak and deerskin
I remember he came to me and took me
rubbed me up, rolled me down
stood me up, put me in his mouth,
tamped me down and pressed me
smooth, rolling me across his lap
his hands were so soothing, soft, mama
warm. We exchanged words him and me
I became full, impregnate at my fine point
his desire flowed   into me —from me
he put me in his mouth laid me back
down, it was quiet on the paper soft bed
I felt water, looked up, tears were falling
I don't know when he'll come again.

Street Walker: Last Time I Seen Cousin Kat

Thomas Park

The girl was thin as a rake; her sweet pie face was grime powdered —ashy emo-eyed.
Lashes broken, black soot speckled her open blouse.

Her brown eyes wanted more than the next hit. She smelled like plastic and Sulfur 8,
her hair was fixed, looked like it was growing.

She looked pulled back like a nappy afro puff. Lazy eye girl.   Quit school and start
hanging with them ill-bred hoboes at that corner store; bumming / smoking.

Now she look like em'...Black eyed girl... down to ninety-two ate-up pounds.
Always bout town begging. At the Chinese diner, cruising the parking lots,

borrowing outside the pizza shop. Cussed me out for asking her not to beg
She be talking shit to people at Rite Aide, selling her EBT benefits.

She barred from the liquor Store, bank, Tea Party headquarters, the community
center, and both gas stations. Her body was by Fisher, now it's by God.

She's anybody's girl for thirty on up. I watched one day; cars come to a stop,
people came and went; drugs flowed on the public lots... Nobody paid attention.

I saw her cop quietly as she could and walk to the woods behind the China King.
The same woods she had babies in—them woods. All she wanted was parents.

Now all girl wants is to hear the sound of the moon slip through the stars,
feel warm blood creep cool-dope through her thin skin, melting her veins.

I saw her cop and walk to the woods with the China King Man.
Anybody's girl for thirty; catch her then she's yours for ten.

The Blue Store in Old Quick City

Thomas Park

Since the cotton mill left for good
all the shotgun tenant houses been moved.
Everything closed, but Newt's Grill

    and the Blue Store.
Yemeni brothers run it but
Half-Ass the chicken frier
owned it. He was mayor's cousin

    and dope man.
Half of his ass was gone
shot off in Viet Nam.
He also ran *Half-Ass*
Handy Man and Wrecker Service,
a boom-boom room way down in the country,
and the smoothest corn I ever tasted.

'Bout dark gap-tooth Clem come to sell snappers
under the poplar trees, by the faded welcome to town sign.
Ol' girl been coming to the spot for years,
her dumb ass man be out fooling with his coon dogs.

Next to Buddy Ro's big cotton field tonight,
two young girls trick with Mexican men behind a bale.
Trips me out when I see the young girls out-there.

On one end of the gravel lot Cholos; gang-bangers,

comparing low-riders, profiling bucks in white tees.
Brothers at the other end floss baseball caps, 10k chains.
Trynna to look hard in sneakers and shit—For what?

To ride high in Crown Vics...it's the same folks every day.
Ate out and ate up the cats smoking in the cut said,
they used to back up the *Chi-Lights.* They was
bad dudes; Fat-Back, Red, and Beans Burton.

Timothy (Timmy)
Thomas Park

   I have slept around.

I've smoked joints with Matthew and Paul.
Slumbered in love with Muhammad in the Quran,
ate cognac over ice cream with Shakespeare,
and nodded on the curb sides while Poe puked.

I've dined with Baldwin in another country,
masturbated in orgy with Bronte and Josephine Baker,
walked alleys with Baudelaire's prostitutes,
fucked Michele in two dreams.

In the spiritual gardens and gully of life
I trickle through, fear rises with agency,
I pick clarity from my iris patch in reds,
content to sleep with whoever I pick up.

everything is a little electric

Giorgia Sage

i fell for her really hard i guess i
fell for her really hard
she tasted like a muggy summer in the mountains
looking up from between her legs i almost told her
"you taste like thunderstorms" but i think i said
"i love you" instead. she said i wasn't allowed to
but it was everywhere you know how
people are everywhere

sex was like scraping your teeth across a mango skin
trying to get all the fruit off and almost not worth the effort but still
impossible to leave unfinished. she always left me
a little unfinished and a little
shaken up. i think she tasted less like
thunderstorms and more like small tart plums
maybe they're the same thing.

i've always been good at landing on my feet
always climb to the top branch. getting down
is the hardest part. but who said you have to?
"get down from there" she told me the last time i saw her
"make me." i wanted to jump but it wasn't high enough
to kill me. just would have hurt a lot and it already did.

i love a few things:
i love ferns. i love mangos. i love mountain storms.
i love static shocks when you cross a carpet and touch a doorknob.

it almost feels like waking up.

i don't need any more of this to know what pain means:
leaving her house at 2am while she is asleep and never looking back.
waking up at 5 in my own room at the same time
she wakes up in hers and texts me "why"

because we're a faulty circuit and i'm tired of stray sparks
because my silence always says more than i mean it to
because i wanted her to fuck me and i said "i love you" instead
and i hate the sound of thunder and i hate the taste of plums

lovebites

Giorgia   Sage

i. i was never any good at geography;

space or time
place or pace
You and me

ii. your hands on my body are hurricanes
i name each touch alphabetically

v. at this point even my heart has charley horses
lathe it with tiger balm. feel it burn

vii. i like thick grass because you never know what is hiding in it

watch out for that snake!

viii. i graze on thoughts of you as horses do on milkweed
toxic and rampant

xi. our bodies together feel like snapping twigs off a branch—
the short ecstasy of it!

xiv. when i'm near you my heart beats how a cat
jumps   suddenly
then not at all

xv. the cows are lowing like church bells down by the river
will they tell me what time it is?

xvii. the field is filled with mustard grass
its yellow blooms are
hundreds of small monks immolating themselves in the sunset

could i catch fire too? a fledgling phoenix, a galloping horse
enormous

xx. all i can think of is the pink head and belly
of a gray bird   and the sound of motorcycles
on a road. You open your eyes slowly in the morning
trees grow in them, and the small sound of laughter.

you are my brief forest.

xxi. i think, what is it like
to be a car going a hundred miles an hour on an empty road?
you are already inside me
and i think, when will I go home?

xxii. as if standing in the middle of a flock of pigeons
taking flight i could see heaven

xxiii. i don't want You in a forever way i just want You
in a right now way that feels like a tire fire
burning for a looong time.

xxvii. SPREAD OUT BENEATH ME LIKE SOME KIND OF FLOODPLAIN
MURKY WATER FULL OF LEECHES
READY TO SUCK YOU DRY SIPHON OFF ALL YOUR RAW POETRY
WHEN YOU LOOK AT ME LIKE WHOAH

I'M BLUE AS A KINGFISHER HAPPY ON
ITS BRANCH. YOU WRITHE AGAINST ME
LIKE A FISH IN MY BEAK.

xxviii. the words i love you sound like a vase to me
something to fill with water and put your flowers in

wreck something

Giorgia Sage

1.

you make me want to eat poison dart frogs
when you tell me the exact number of miles
between where each of us will be six months from now

i file my canine teeth in your bathroom mirror before you wake
preparing myself for the fight i know is coming
creep back into bed, my cold soles against your warm calves

you stir, mouthing at my collarbone
with your hands on my skin
i quiver like a kicked dog
caught between moving closer and away

2.
you are—

não tenho fluência suficiente em qualquer linguagem
*dirti come sento**

am i frothing at the mouth yet?

tie me up outside in your backyard
watch me wreck something

3.
in my dreams, *you lock me, still damp*
in a blue cupboard
i grow moldy, sprout clumps of phosphorescent mushrooms

you go mushroom picking on my body
sit at my red kitchen table, i in my
wet blue cupboard

i watch as you eat
and begin to glow
you drink tap water and blink. the sound of knives and forks
distill themselves in the space in front of you

i wake and get out of bed
standing in your bathroom i wash my face with cold water
i sharpen my canines

how hungry i am.

*i don't have enough fluency in any language to tell you how i feel

you are like
Giorgia   Sage

my head is swirling, full
swirling out my eyes
in all the ways i looked at you

when you walked in the door of the coffee shop
i knocked my soda over. it fizzed into my jeans
as you looked at me like my clumsiness was a secret
you wanted whispered in your ear.

when you slid into the booth beside me
pressing your thigh against mine
you wiped up the soda with a wad of napkins
and ordered a garden burger

after all your struggles to climb
into the cave of my skull
you found yourself already there,
hanging upside down
your skin as translucent as the wing of a bat

"life is a lot," i say
that night under your duvet

you ask me to explain
i can't because i always say
as much as I know
which isn't very much at all

i am still trying to learn how to ask the questions
your scratched legs coming through the blackberry bushes behind
        my house
through the haze of early morning

"you are a lot,"
i don't even say it as you gingerly pull my shirt over my head
i'm too busy gasping into the space
between your shoulder and neck
as you suck the blackberry from my fingertips

i try to inflate you like a helium balloon
with words so big you float up and
bob against my ceiling, glowing and full
so i can watch you like a constellation
as i fall asleep

Je Tiens A Vous Faire Pleurer A Dieu et Ce Sera Moi Qui Reponds

Phillip   Sroka

for Isidore Ducasse

An ant hill on top of a mountain is
little consolation when considering
the piercing coal-choked cry that
tears into the sky. One could only
wonder:

Is it the Papaver or heroine they are after?

> When the ends are all the same
> it is only a matter of how many
> each one of us has buggered.

A steam engine barrels 95 down
a lateral embankment that may
or may not end in disaster. The conversation
within the dining car revolves around
the ideology of time while someone
else unbuttons Suzy's saddle. (Sub-
urban punks will lament a Banksy
on the north face of the fourth car.)

I wish I were the keeper of those buttons.

Ants offer poor comparison when it comes
to men. They work so well that it leaves
little room for error (approximation).

To the hill tops we march with our
bundles of taffeta, trailing buttons as we
scale the deep fur incline.
We make camp. Light a smoke.
Pat each other on the back.

 The Pleiades shine so well sometimes.

We knit and grunt simultaneously
a darling communion dress. (I imagine
caressing each button between
the salivation of my tongue and thighs.) We moan
like cloistered satyrs with each cross stitch.

     Suzy likes ant farms far more
     than she could ever tell. She
     shakes them in private and
     watches them choke on chenille.

Our laughs stain red the dew that whisks
away the evidence of our presence
on the mountain. Except of course for the train,
only it remains a dead centipede disassembled
by the ants.

(Translation of title: "I want to make you cry to God and it will be me who answers.")

For Your Studies

Bethany Tap

"What happens when we die?" Bobby asked his mother Shirley. At seven, Bobby imagined Grandpa Bob suddenly inhabiting a spirit world made of Jell-O.

Shirley put her arm around him. Bobby frowned. Shirley wasn't affectionate. Usually, she would burst into the room, bits of froth stuck on her lips, yelling at him to "keep it down" or "do your homework," often adding, "you piece of shit."

Now, Shirley told Bobby about heaven, a place where "the part of you that makes you who you are goes to be with Jesus."

Bobby's frown deepened because Shirley's hand was stroking his arm. He placed his palm on hers and lifted it, like he would lift his garter snake, Billie Jean. Bobby wanted to be an ophiologist; he would study snakes.

Shirley hated snakes. She didn't know about Billie Jean, whom Grandpa Bob had found on one of their expeditions.

"For your ophiology studies," Grandpa Bob said, handing Billie Jean to Bobby.

"What about mom?" Bobby asked. "She'll kill me!"

"Then don't tell her!" Grandpa said, as if it were easy, which it turned out to be.

Bobby kept Billie Jean in his closet, her cage tucked under a pile of old clothes that Shirley was too lazy to take to Goodwill. Bobby figured Billie Jean was safe.

Now, Shirley glared at Bobby. "Aren't you sad, Robert Harris? Christ, I thought you loved your grandpa!"

Bobby did love his grandpa. Maybe even more than Billie Jean. He thought about Shirley's speech and wondered what part of Grandpa had made him Grandpa.

"How did he die?" Bobby asked before Shirley walked out of the room.

"Aneurysm."

"What's that?"

"It means his brain stopped working."

But wasn't that the part of Grandpa that made him Grandpa? It wasn't his liver-spotted hands or his scent, like cinnamon and cigarettes. It was his brain, the way he thought and the words he said.

After Shirley left, Bobby went into the closet to feed Billie Jean. He told her about Grandpa Bob. She seemed sad; she only ate one of the baby mice he'd brought.

Bobby felt hot anger pulse through him. Grandpa Bob had promised to take him fishing that weekend, but now he was a head floating in Jell-O. Worse. He didn't have a head. Grandpa Bob had given him Billie Jean. Bobby hated Billie Jean. She reminded him of hikes in the woods, canoe rides, shooting practice, and everything Bobby loved that was gone.

"What happens when we die, Billie Jean?"

She closed her eyes.

"That's right," Bobby nodded. "Nothing." He raised his fist and brought it down with a crack onto Billie Jean's skull. The snake fell limp like a broken promise. The part of Billie Jean that made her Billie Jean was destroyed.

Bobby wanted to cry, but didn't. He buried Billie Jean in the backyard and wondered if she was cold down there. Then he remembered she was dead. She couldn't feel anything. There was nothing to feel.

Issue 4: Winter/Spring 2015

(Cover Art: Barbara Ruth)

Introduction: The Doors of Perception

Welcome to Issue 4! We invite you, reader, to open — or perhaps cleanse — your "Doors of Perception".

We must have to admit, the fault lies first on William Blake for this issue's theme. Well known is his quote from *The Marriage of Heaven and Hell*:

"If the doors of perception were cleansed every thing would appear to man as it is, Infinite."

This quote inspired both Aldous Huxley in his classic work "The Doors of Perception" and a young Jim Morrison to name the rock band he helped found — The Doors. Thus, Huxley and Morrison are also to blame for our choice for this issue's theme. Thus, we dedicate Issue 4 to Blake, Huxley, Morrison, and also to the other three members of The Doors — John Densmore, Robbie Krieger, and the late Ray Manzarek.

We considered the idea that humans are called to challenge their perceptions of life and sometimes reality itself. Psychological factors, our own opinions, prejudices, and mental filters can alter and severely cloud the way we see reality around us. It is up to each one of us to choose for ourselves how we see reality — and through what lenses.

In the last quarter of 2014, a clarion call was issued to the world, and to Western society in particular, to cleanse its "doors of perception" in many areas, including: waking up and seeing realities of racism. and police violence. as evidenced by the deaths of Michael Brown, Tamir Rice, and Eric Garner, to name a few; recognising the growing number of transgender and non-binary gender individuals suffering. and dying. as a result of transphobia, such as Leelah Alcorn and Islan Nettles; and challenging the public perception fueled by Autism Speaks of autistic individuals as tragedies, missing people, and burdens to their families.

We asked for poetry, artwork, and short fiction which interpreted our chosen theme as broadly or as narrowly as desired: we received an amazing outpouring of work and it was difficult to decide what pieces to choose for this issue. This was a good problem to have, but delayed the issue's release a wee bit. We hope that the extra time we have taken to carefully consider and select the poems, fiction, and artwork is reflected in both the quality and the emotional impact of Issue 4.

Longtime *Barking Sycamores* contributor Barbara Ruth is our cover artist for this issue. One of her short fiction pieces will appear in this issue as well as four other photomanipulation art pieces.

Thank you again for reading. We appreciate all of your support as we publish our fourth issue, and are looking forward to another year of featuring work by neurodivergent writers and artists. Keep watching! More is headed your way.

Family Portrait
Heather Dorn

My father insists he's Italian by arguing
with my husband over the pronunciation
of food items. Instead of therapy, he suggests
I yell at him (for watching him hit my mother
he never says). My mother brags she's Swedish
by pulling at my 8 year old braids to tuck them in dog-ears
for St. Lucia's Day. She tells me it doesn't hurt me, like when
she tightens the loops of my braces for the dentist. One day
she'll throw a frying pan at her ex-husband. My brother
showed he's related by banging his head into the floor
until he bled and cutting his wrists later. There is
nothing in us that doesn't want out of the body
like blood.

❖   ❖   ❖

How to Be Manic
Heather Dorn

Talk loudly about how much you love to dance
or even louder about how you hate your mother
in law. When your friends ask you to lower your
voice, tell them to 'fuck off.' Sing every song as if

you were the artist. Believe it's something you
could really do, after all you did 6th grade choir
and a musical in high school. Decide to become

a singer and actress. Decide to dress in your high

school clothes. The skirt won't zip up so untuck
the shirt. Lie in bed and wait for your husband
or your boyfriend or your girlfriend or have an
affair. Have sex and then have sex and then have

a speed down the highway because you will never
die. After all, you haven't yet and so you can't. Decide
maybe you're not human. Maybe you are something
else. Maybe you can sprout cat ears and a tail for balance.

Maybe you can limp along fence posts and blend
with the night. Maybe you can become invisible
before jumping into the sun and lying in a beam.
Feel a rumble in your belly that won't go away.

It rumbles in your head. Throw a rusted training
wheel down your driveway, drink too much Scotch
to slow your thoughts. Remember how much you hate
yourself. Think it might be sensible to cut yourself

and let the anger leak out. Practice on your pinky
to see how deep you can make yourself go. Make it
a contest. Make it up to yourself with vodka when you
get tired of creating new finger prints.

The Time Traveler

Heather Dorn

There's not as much jam these days on bread he said
leaning into his idea. *And all the soap comes off your*
skin in seconds. He liked the concept of lingering
so he sat down in the square to prove a theory. A dog
who wanted company made a deal for some stale rolls
and the traveler had his team assembled. Supplies
in order too: blankets, mat, brush, backpack. And the weather
though hot, was pleasant enough, as he watched

a family use the swing set at the park across the road —
two kids in the saddle and a couple pushing them. The girl
in braids looked like her antennae were being swirled up
into a tornado and the tornado had already taken her
front teeth. And she screamed as she fell from the sky
and begged for the next close call of gravity to pull her in.

The traveler noted this in his book with his index finger
and decided that the Sun was keeping a grudge on him
and was trying to make things hotter. He chanted "Pan-pan...
pan-pan...pan-pan..." and flapped his outstretched arms
up and down, waiting for his signal to get through. People
around him averted their eyes and gave him wing space.
The girl across the street jumped off her swing and flapped her arms,
singing, "Pans!" The traveler thought she must be the first
of her kind to see him and he kept flapping, hoping that
if they both sent the message, someone might pick up
on his distress signs.

What Type of Person Are You?: Take the Quiz!

Heather Dorn

You Got: Marzipan person with a metal knife hidden inside. You got: Most likely to be stood up, sitting at the bar at *Zippers*. You got: Diseased. You got: No shoulder pads. You got: Still awake at 6 a.m., writing poems for the trash, clothes all over your floor and a piece of pizza on your night stand. No plate. You got: Left alone all weekend as a child, green bean dinner, powdered milk, the apartment has Skinimax, "Weekend at Bernie's" plays so often you memorize it, you don't know the names of the other movies, you don't listen to the words. You got: Watch "Embrace of the Vampire" so often you fall in love with Alyssa Milano. And vampires. You got: *Jane Eyre* means everything. You got: Folders, binders, pens, pencils, markers, flash drives, crayons, notebooks. You got: Buy everything. You got: Alice in Wonderland, DRINK ME. You got: Sick: one day hitting a curb and a stop sign in slow motion, 2 miles an hour, tied to a hospital bed by oxygen tubes up your nose, heart trying to die, no salt, no salt, watch your water intake too, no alcohol anymore, walk because running will bleed everything through. You got: Drunk and running in the street, bleeding energy from every surface, red wine spilling all over your white dress.

Dear John

Jessica   Goody

The line between tacky and chic pulled taut,
your hair dyed: comic book heroine yellow.
You, unfortunately, are the victim, not the savior.

Crimson talons, hard edges fraying
the chasm between cheapness and glamour.
You know it well: local beers more bitter
with swallowed tongue than sour hops.
Rough sheets on rented beds chafe
skin that longs to remain tender

Bloody lipstick meant to evoke sophistication
only camouflages (somewhat)
the inevitable split lip,
or the puffed and vivid shiner.

Too bad you cannot be candid at funerals.
You must clench your teeth, force tears
(you were forced that night; the tears came on their own).
You cannot speak in italic fonts,
words lurching drunkenly (as he did) with emotion,
words underscored and highlighted with pain.

No spat exclamations,
words writhing like serpents on the tongue,
flung with force, a verbal grenade.
You cannot stomp on the gravesite,
cannot spit into the void where the shining box
will soon be lowered.

You cannot scream, cannot
clip the blossoms from the roses
and toss the thorny stems,
ragged with abuse, into the pit.
All around you, dark-clad strangers
are weeping decorously,
and you wonder who it is, exactly,
that they are referring to:

"Loving father."
No, not that, never to you.
You can only hope that he smooths
his daughter's pretty gold hair,
swings her in the air, and exclaims over
her crayoned pictures:

a lopsided nuclear family (a perfect metaphor),
joyful Fido, a green-grassed blue-skied life
where it never rains except to sate the flowers
and that rain is never heavy, cold, gloomy,
or bears thunder, a child's nightmare soundtrack.

"Devoted husband"? Doubtful,
as he was there that night,
branding your wrists with plummy bruises,
joyfully violent.
Standing here, you wonder

how this man, a fine upstanding citizen,
so well-liked that the local paper gave
page room for his obituary,
and the Kiwanis, the Elks, the VFW Hall

sent roses. Red, like the blood he left on your lip.
Red, like his bloodshot eyes.

Learning to Walk

Jessica   Goody

Trembling beneath woolen blankets,
you cannot get warm as you shiver from
ague's aftershock. There is no warning,
no indication among the sickroom paraphernalia:
enamel basins and iron cots,
a burning mustard plaster, the scent of wet wool.
The mercury stretches, rising in the feverish glass.

Released from the iron lung's bathysphere,
that claustrophobic cage,
your legs are foreign, rigid as a cadaver:
dead weights, flaccid as flour sacks.
Your disconnected telephone switchboard nerves
struggle to speak: no response, no dial tone.

Pristinely white twin casts of humid plaster
are cracked like lobster shells,
pried from withered, aching limbs.
Tourniquet-taut leather straps dig into fragile skin
as orthotics' iron exoskeleton is locked into place.

The clanking armor of shackles and scaffolding
weighs down straining muscles, sandbag-heavy limbs
that sweat in the clumsy waltz of left-right, scrape and drag:

each painful step you tread like a fakir over hot coals
in your knuckle-white struggle to remain upright.

Migraines
Jessica   Goody

Struggling against nausea's rising tide,
I brace myself against wind blasting
through the open window: the cool air, a distraction.
My muscles strain against my roiling stomach,
tightening, forcing the bitter bile into place.

This profound discomfort consumes the mind,
requiring every focus in every cell and pore.
The throat constricts, the body fighting
against the release of poisonous bile.
It emerges, spreading, a fierce yellow.
My organs tense, cramping deeply, ejecting every drop.

The intensity of the reflex burns my throat.
Emptied and gagging, the spasms persist:
digestive convulsions leave me weak and perspiring.
My body keeps draining itself of all fluid.
Consumed by the ferocity of the siege,
I am trembling. My eyes stream of their own accord;
I am too preoccupied to be embarrassed.

Dry as a cornhusk, my bones ache
with emptiness. My equilibrium has been shattered.
The world shudders around me; it is not solid

beneath my fingertips. These neurological tremblings,
little tremors, tiny flesh earthquakes
leave me afraid of the world, left without survival skills,
groping for safety in empty spaces.
My only refuge: the white nest of my bed.

❖   ❖   ❖

COOL IN THE GREY FALL NIGHT, Michael Lee Johnson

Dead Grey Wolf Skins

Michael Lee Johnson

1935.
Dead grey wolf skins hang
on white clotheslines across Baraboo, Wisconsin
the dark surface, dirty old shack, side of the moon,

that only exists in memories hung high, long before.
Hunters in the past did their job well,
sold skins, collected a few bucks,
increased deer for hunting, saved cattle,
decreased fear, told tales, short stories, adventures.

The grey wolf face now emergent,
opens his mouth wide in the safety
open in blue sky.
Shows his white teeth against
background of black sky, shadow,
hears thunder again, releases
fireflies at night, monarch butterflies
during the day, guts down pine tree spikes.
He walks once again over landscapes of turquoises.
He consumes dirt road dust, tracks trails,
114.4 miles from Milwaukee to Baraboo.
His keen eyes are sharp for growth
of skyscraper, Pabst brewery building.
Traveling side roads over many years brings him to the present.
No more violators, hunters with guns, fake Jesus people
slender in His bathrobe Christ repeats two fishes, 5 loaves
and the wolf survives.

Aldo Leopold feeding inmate in small jail cells,
only kills a few wolves for research.
Aldo a Saint of conservation a consumer of cigarettes and butts,
heart wings of doves attached, broken, stroke fire, a neighbor field
heart stroke drops into history.

Author's Note: *This poem is a tribute to* **Aldo Leopold** *(January 11, 1887 — April 21, 1948), an American author, scientist, ecologist,* *forester, environmentalist, and conservationist. In the 1920-1930 eras, he moved to the Baraboo, Wisconsin area. The grey wolf was viewed as a predator, to be killed and sold for their skins. Even then, the grey wolf population was diminishing. Leopold helped restore the value and dignity of the grey wolf to Wisconsin farmers and residents.*

If You Find No Poem

Michael   Lee   Johnson

If you find
no poem on
your doorstep
in the morning,
no paper, no knock on your door,
your life poorly edited
but no broken dashes
or injured meter-

if you do not wear white
satin dresses late in life
embroidered with violet
flowers on the collar;
nor do you have
burials daily
across main street-

if no one whispers
in your ear, Emily Dickinson-
you feel alone-
but not reclusive-

the sand child
still sleeping in your eyes-
wiping your tears away-

if you find
no poem on
your doorstep-
you know
you are not from New England.

Poem of Sinners and Saints

Michael Lee Johnson

Sinners hurt.
While moonlight cracks open
like a walnut, spreads soft light across open sky,
they dart to alleyways, bury themselves behind
their own trails shaking fists at the sky;
hiding their nasty nonsense in shame,
city buildings rattle their bricks, mortar loose at their rib cage.

All men think they are sword men daggers in darkness.
All women think they are entry points leaning against brick walls,
slender on sidewalks past midnight,
nothing but shadows, twitching of lips.
Women look for drawing cards in their makeup kits.
No one cares jackals, scavengers, men tempted by night.
Thunder dreams hammer at their ears,
rain urinate sins on street corners,
mice crawl away to small places shamed.

Early morning crows fly.
Footsteps scatter directions as sunlight sprouts.
Misdeeds carry no names with them
they trip blind, racing to morning jobs.
Sin hurts staples in women's lungs,
staples dagger in men's ribs.

Schizophrenia Night

Michael   Lee   Johnson

I am a chalkboard computer brain.
I have updated drawn raw
images even the classroom
students cannot see, hear, nor understand.
They sit quietly in Disneyland
wondering about my eccentricities
I capture their stillness, and then I speak.
I am the professor, special agent of government
dream tracer of crossroad puzzles.
Photographic memory in private rooms,
did I hear a critic, erase
destroy dissociate thoughts.
I walk out unsteady in disbelief.
Is there a shadow of storybooks following me?

I am a genius; I know who I am.
I spend nights in formula construction
drawing full color images of my brain,
percentages of gray matter lost.

I stick my ego to the bird eagle of the sky.

When on a high on an airplane, self-love,
full bloom, I keep my enemies at bay.
I shelter the skeletons of thought.

I trust Jesus because His image is stable,
every group I have ever known says "The Lord's Prayer."
Even then, new members leave, disappear, I hear what they said.
I had an MRI to trace all my youthful abuses.
There were no images there but voices I remember.
I cast their shadows, audio, visual for show, in the background.
In time, they quiet their voices. I walk beyond their images.
I pass on, they still screenplay.

You have to stretch lean, refer to sanity,
drink Asian tea, smooth out, limejuice, hallucinated sounds
before that stage, I took that Nobel prize,
even before, I forgave you.

> **Author's Note:** *This poem is devoted to John Nash, the subject of the 2001 movie **A Beautiful Mind**. John Nash has suffered most of his life with severe paranoid schizophrenia and has gone on to be a celebrated American mathematician whose works in game theory, and differential geometry are appreciated around the world. The movie **A Beautiful Mind** portrays Nash's mathematical genius and his struggles with schizophrenia and how he went on to win a Nobel Prize.*

[Decentralized editing]

Craig Kurtz

prompts paradoxical nonessential.
Allicient properties convey
inconclusive chronology.
It wasn't me. Potentiation
to radical category. Take
redirected, & test.

Deregulated language palette
suggests unobstructed. Not
quite. Thoughts perambulate
in aliquots, divagate pro-
miscuously. Etymology
is destiny.

Defenestrate the status quo
& eviscerate epistemology.
Sounds like fun. Proceed w/
irregularity, the consuetude
is in the details. Evolution's
due for an oil change.

Decentralized destiny is
in the redirected. Radical
aliquots divagate test.
Paradoxical epistemology
suggests allicient
irregularity.

Have a Nice Century

Craig   Kurtz

"All tyrannies involve the supposedly perfect understanding of someone else's needs."
— Adam Phillips

If there was perfection
it would be totalitarian.
If you were absolutely right
what would you ever learn?
Now is the moment to concede
impossible colors coexist.

I don't want a time machine;
I am my own metronome.
However much you collect
you only keep what you create.
Now is the time to suppose
maybe no one ever knows.

If there was global happiness
it would be the end of progress.
If your dreams all came true
someone would be unemployed.
Now could be the occasion
to question your own recognition.

I don't want a crystal ball; I'll take
my chances w/ the shape of smoke.
However much control gets achieved
stop signs stop working when we sleep.
There was an instant no one assayed:

Flying children forgot they could not.

Reasons
Craig   Kurtz

Where is the planet
where there are reasons
instead of contradictions.
Where are the people
who understand me
instead of confound
my expectations.
& who do I address
when I ask why?

Where is the planet
where there are answers
instead of errors.
Where are the inhabitants
who might make sense
of these dilemmas known
as people making people.
& who would I choose
to decide?

Where is the planet
worth the wait for questions
that hasten more conjecture.
Where does the discovery
of certainty go when it's
true only the new is

never unknown.
& why do I think I
know what I anticipate?

Tin Foil World
Craig Kurtz

Since when
did democracy
become the reason
you're not wanting
what you get.

Since when
did fair is fair become
why the starting gate
got hurry up & wait
the way it is.

There's a breakdown
in reception.

Since when
did that's always how
become the solution
instead of the problem
right from go.

Since when
started now you know

the premise instead of
the end point so figure
the trigger out.

There's rows of voices
over every roof.

Plague Year

A.J. Odasso

So far, we've had

a shattered ankle

deaths in the family

a case of dengue fever:

this plague falls on

just and kind alike.

When the phone rings

or a new message lands,

I reach with chilled fingers,

gather still life in my hands.

Meanwhile, my world in its
corner is quiet. Twig tea and
the sweeping of dust are my
only concerns. Out there,
howling wild, letters swirl in
digital miasma or as sound
waves and reach my door. I
am their switchboard, gate-
keeper to an afterlife in which
doctors' notes and funeral
notices are more postscript
than prayer. I love them as I
love my own soul: those I
cannot save, I forward to
another desk scrubbed of
blood, another stamp of fate.

Some of them return,

tell sordid tales and smile,

eyes bright with forgetting

that they crossed an ocean

while they were sleeping,

did not know they dreamed

they might pay in marrow

and scripted flesh: my palms,

they cross with forgiveness;

coins, I press to their tongues.

Whose Dream?

Barbara Ruth

"If you don't have the test we'll have to give you the medication for both viral and bacterial meningitis, plus medication for encephalitis," Dr. Chen said. I took a peek at her face, then looked away; her eyes behind her thick glasses made me dizzy. "If you don't actually have those diseases, you're taking the medicines unnecessarily."

"Aren't you already giving me Keflax for the UTI? Won't that knock out whatever I've got?"

"No." She shook her head and the motion made me shut my eyes in self-defense.

"I'm refusing treatment," I announced. I tried to sit up a little, the more vertical you get, the more authority you have. "I know I have the right legally to refuse a lumbar puncture, and I do take meningitis seriously. I'm willing to take the medications, I think that's a reasonable precaution." Did the 5150 mean I lost the right to refuse treatment? I wasn't sure.

"All right, we'll do it that way then," Dr. Chen said. "I'll write the order and your first treatment will be tonight."

Night. The time when there were no more visitors. The time when I could hear the deep bass notes, deeper than any sound the hospital made, the vibration of the earth turning on its axis. The Dalai Lama visited me, and this was a dream, clearly a dream, not channeling, not his voice in my head, a regular, everybody gets them, dream.

The Dalai Lama showed me around my hospital gown and the hospital bed. I didn't know how to find my way in either, but it turns out they both have hidey-holes, places most people can't see, places to hang on to, to make your way around, or at least, turn and sit up just a bit.

The hospital was so noisy. I missed music, oh I yearned for music. I'd heard a few people whistle or hum to themselves and my ears followed,

followed, far down the halls and into the elevators to remain with the music. I opened my eyes. Dr. Chen had gone. Had I drifted off?

The nurse came in, shift change. "Esme! I thought you'd be gone longer. I'm so glad to see you."

She pulled on the overhead wraparound curtains as she came toward me. "I'm glad to see you too, Π. You don't need these anymore?"

"I do! I need my blue around me. The light hurts my eyes so bad, and looking makes me dizzy." I was grateful SOMEBODY who worked here knew my name, asked me questions that mattered to me, questions I could answer.

She drew the cocoon back around me, blue curtains curving around all the sides, making a circle. She rolled up close to me on her rolling stool with a clipboard on her lap. "Tell me how you've been." What was that accent? I didn't know, maybe Central American, maybe Chinese? I loved the melody of her voice, just wanted to follow that and not have to pay attention to the lyrics. She didn't insist I make words out loud, just continued, "Let me examine you then." She took my blood pressure with her own sphygmomanometer. "Oh my," she said, looking up and down my arms. "So many more bruises from IVs than when I saw you last time. I'll get warm compresses when I finish this."

Her touch quieted me. The janitor came and went with his cleaning supplies but I felt protected by Esme and the special healing tent she'd made me, even though I knew it couldn't keep out smells. Could I just pretend I was sick at the Michigan Womyn's Music Festival and they took me to the Womb, the healing tent, and even though it was barely quieter than the area all around, after all, the tent was only canvas, just the same, inside I would feel so protected. They would drum my breath back to me, and there would be massage and music therapy. Someone would know healing modes, like I used to try to compose myself. I did that, I wrote music and poetry. An Irish bard, Daddy said. He was proud of me, and truly he didn't care that I never made a decent living. Could I make a decent dying? Was that time coming?

Esme would understand why I refused the lumbar puncture, after all the botched blood draws and IVs. I tried to smile and the cannula bumped out of my nose. Esme repositioned it, tucking the cord up under my chin.

"I know lot of the people who work here think I'm difficult," I told her. "And I realize my sensitivities to smells and noise don't go with the bustle of a hospital. I know people can't always accommodate me. I'd leave if I could."

"Don't worry about it," Esme said. "I understand. We're here to take care of you. I'm going to do everything I can to make this hospital as comfortable for you as possible as long as you're on my station."

I asked Esme for ice chips. The cold jolted the inside of my mouth.

My fingers are cold. I am sitting here telling you about what happened to me, through the story of a character I made up named Π. Wow, was it ever hard, just now, to reach up into OpenOffice, and find Π under "Insert" under "special letters", "alphabets", "basic Greek."

I go back there now. I go into the hospital once a week and I read the records for one hour. Then I wander the halls where I was incarcerated/kept alive/nearly killed. Now you know how the story comes out! Now you know Π didn't die, though I'm thinking about killing her off. After all, this is a work of fiction.

What if this is Π's dream? What if this is Esme's dream, or Dr. Chen's? Whose dream. Are you.

Author's Notes: *This piece is an excerpt from her autobiographical novel* Lying In Beds I Never Made.

The author also provides a definition for "5150" from **Wikipedia**: *Section 5150 is a section of the California Welfare and Institutions Code which authorizes a qualified officer or clinician to involuntarily confine a person suspected to have a mental disorder that makes him or her a danger to themselves, a danger to others, and/or gravely disabled. Colloquially used as noun ("this person is a 5150") or verb ("she was 5150ed.")*

Mikey Allcock

FORT #1

FORT #2

Robin Como

OPEN DOOR

Robin Como

UP THE STAIRS

Chris McLean

SOUNDGARDENS #1

Barbara Ruth

FEARFUL SYMMETRY

Barbara Ruth

SOMETIMES THEY BARK LIKE THIS

Barbara Ruth

TOO MANY EYES

Barbara Ruth

WHALE WATCHING IN SAN JOSE

Contributors

Sarah Akin

Sarah Akin was born in 1979. She's a lifelong Massachusetts resident and currently resides in New Bedford, Massachusetts with her boyfriend (George) and their Lynx Point Siamese. She's as Autistic as the day is long and eternally grateful for the support of the neurodiverse community.

◆   ◆   ◆

Mikey Allcock

Born in 1998, Mikey was diagnosed with autism before he was 2 years old. At the age of 10 he began to talk and write. At 12 he started to play the piano and is now an accomplished pianist. In June 2014, aged 16, he started to paint. His artwork has been published in the press, the *Autism File* journal and also accepted for publication in *The Art of Autism's* 2016 calendar.

◆   ◆   ◆

Samm Almester

Samm Almester is an undergraduate college student in northwest Ohio, majoring in the digital arts. They are nineteen years old, and have autism, depression, and anxiety (afflicted with trichotillomania, as a result). They also are transgender, more specifically non-binary (agender) and use they/them pronouns. Their personal website is gendercosmos.tumblr.com.

◆   ◆   ◆

Emily Paige Ballou

Emily Paige Ballou has degrees in drama and biology from the University of Georgia. She currently lives and works in New York City as an Off-Broadway and new media stage manager. Diagnosed with Asperger's in her 20's, she is a volunteer for the Autism Women's Network, co-editor of the blog *We Are Like Your Child*, and has had other writing published in *Stick Your Neck Out*, *Shift Journal*, and *NeuroQueer*.

♦ ♦ ♦

Amy Barlow Liberatore

Amy Barlow Liberatore is a poet, singer/songwriter, and activist. She writes about politics, mental divergence, and her maternal Irish family. Amy is vocal about living with manic depression and PTSD as well as surviving childhood sexual abuse; she's also been an ally of the LGBTQ community since age five!   She lives in Madison, WI, with her husband, Lex; daughter Laura Weinberger is an LA-based artist.   Amy sings rowdy music in church, prays for peace, works for justice, and writes her own truth.

She blogs at sharplittlepencil.com.

♦ ♦ ♦

Matthew Brown

Matthew Brown has been writing poetry for 46 years, and although he doesn't have an official diagnosis, he came to the conclusion that he has Asperger's from doing research, after his daughter told a college counselor her life story, and the counselor suggested that her dad might have Asperger's.

It is certainly true that he has always perceived the world and reality differently from most others, and was often persecuted or "tolerated" for that as a child and young person. He also had some of the typical traits, such as shaking his hands violently when excited by something, things he learned to suppress in public.

He graduated from Saginaw Valley State University in 1976, and is working on an MFA in poetry at Ashland University. Matthew has always worked in factories, shops, apartment complexes and so on because he has no orientation towards a career in the normal sense.

He has been married to Kay Elizabeth Brown since 1982, and has a daughter, a son, and two grandsons.

◆　◆　◆

Cathy Carlisi

Cathy Carlisi's poetry has appeared in *Prairie Schooner, The Atlanta Review, The Mid-American Review, Southern Review* and many others. She is President, Chief Creative Officer at BrightHouse, a consultancy that serves organizations that serve society.

◆　◆　◆

Ellie Castellanos

Ellie Castellanos is a 15 year-old autistic artist currently residing in Alamo, CA with her family. Ellie has been creating original artwork since the age of three. She is self-trained but is studying art in school with the hope of someday supporting herself through her artwork. Ellie's interest in art is widespread. She is interested primarily in sculpture, digital art, photography, and stop motion animation.

A sample of her work can be seen at her website: http://www.elliecastellanos.com.

◆   ◆   ◆

Tasha Chemel

Tasha Chemel is a teacher, poet, and potter. She refers to herself as transabled (physically blind, but sighted-identified). Her loves include critical theory, fanfiction, and yoga. She received her Master's in Education from Harvard University. She lives in Cambridge, Massachusetts.

◆   ◆   ◆

Deanna Christian

Deanna Christian is a retired technical editor and English teacher. She is from the Pacific Northwest and is now happily retired in Bowling Green, KY where new Mennonite friends are teaching her to bake amazing pies and homemade bread. She is also a colored pencil artist; you can see her work on DeannaChristian.Weebly.com

◆   ◆   ◆

Robin Como

Robin Como is a Pennsylvania writer, poet, editor, and photographer boldly seeking to document the satirical. Her poetry appeared in *Beatdom* magazine and she writes for magazines and newspapers. She recently edited "I Consider It My Duty," a two-volume book on the War of 1812. You can find her on Twitter: https://twitter.com/comophone.

◆   ◆   ◆

Allen Davis

Allen X. Davis' short fiction appears in *Madcap Review, Microfiction Monday, A Quiet Courage,* and *Empty Sink Publishing.* He works for a bank and is an avid photographer.

♦   ♦   ♦

Melissa DeHart

Melissa DeHart is an undergraduate student at Florida State University, studying Editing, Writing, and Media and International Affairs. She works as a freelance editor and proofreader, and in her spare time she writes fictional stories.

♦   ♦   ♦

Heather Dorn

Heather Dorn is the Director of the Binghamton Poetry Project, a literary outreach providing free poetry workshops to the community. She will graduate with her PhD in Creative Writing Spring 2016. Her poems have appeared in the *Paterson Literary Review, Ragazine,* the *Kentucky Review* and similar journals.

♦   ♦   ♦

fayola

Fayola (Lindsey Anderson) is a neurodivergent, queer activist raised in the South. Lindsey is a teacher at the Ala Costa Adult Transition Program in Berkeley, California where she works with neurodivergent adults learning neurodiversity advocacy as well as vocational and travel skills. Her most current project creates accessible formats of neurodivergent history intentionally recorded and translated by neurodivergent people.

◆　◆　◆

Leila Fortier

Leila A. Fortier is a Pushcart Prize nominated poet, artist, and photographer residing in Okinawa, Japan. She is a member of the Alpha Sigma Lambda National Honor Society; pursuing her BFA in creative writing through Southern New Hampshire University. Her sculpted poetry is often accompanied by her own multi-medium forms of art, photography, and spoken performance. Known for her contributions to humanitarian causes through the arts, selections of her work have also been translated into French, Italian, Spanish, Arabic, and German in a growing effort to foster cultural diversity and understanding through the voice of poetry. She has most recently initiated the venue Poetic License to support other writers through book reviews, feature interviews, articles, and inspiration. Her work in all its mediums has been featured in hundreds of publications globally in print and online. *Numinous* is her second book of poetry newly released through Saint Julian Press. A complete listing of her published works can be found at: www.leilafortier.com.

◆　◆　◆

Kimberly Gerry Tucker

Kimberly Gerry Tucker is an artist, writer, carer and autist (diagnosed with Aspergers in 1999.) She is passionate about neurodiversity acceptance and interested in studies of the brain (what makes us all 'tick'?). She enjoys painting, writing (her blog is found at ravenambition.wordpress.com) reading, mosaics, pets, and wrote a book about her experiences with 'growing up on the spectrum and losing a partner to terminal disease. Her book *Under The Banana Moon (living, loving and Aspergers)* can be found on Amazon.

◆　◆　◆

Jessica Goody

Jessica Goody writes for *SunSations Magazine* and *The Bluffton Sun*. Her work has appeared in numerous publications and anthologies, including *Chicken Soup for the Soul, Broad!, Spectrum, Barking Sycamores, HeART, Gravel, PrimalZine, Kaleidoscope, Open Minds Quarterly,* and *Wordgathering*. Her poem "Stockings" was awarded second place in the 2015 *Reader's Digest* Poetry Competition.

◆　◆　◆

Elizabeth J. (Ibby) Grace

Elizabeth J. (Ibby) Grace is an Autistic professor who blogs at tinygracenotes.blogspot.com and edits for i.e.: inquiry in education, NeuroQueer and Autonomous Press. Interested in performance and disability studies, Ibby is working on a musicology book with Andrew Dell'Antonio and a monograph on theater. She currently serves on the board of Society for Disability Studies.

♦   ♦   ♦

Michael Lee Johnson

Michael Lee Johnson lived ten years in Canada during the Vietnam era. He is a Canadian and USA citizen. Today he is a poet, freelance writer, amateur photographer, small business owner in Itasca, Illinois. He has been published in more than 850 small press magazines in 27 countries, and he edits 10 poetry sites. His author's website is http://poetryman.mysite.com/.

Michael is the author of The *Lost American: From Exile to Freedom (136 page book, ISBN: 978-0-595-46091-5),* several chapbooks of poetry, including *From Which Place the Morning Rises* and *Challenge of Night and Day, and Chicago Poems.* He also has over 85 poetry videos on YouTube as of 2015 at https://www.youtube.com/user/poetrymanusa/videos. Michael was also nominated for 2 Pushcart Prize awards for poetry 2015 and currently has several chapbooks in the works.

♦   ♦   ♦

Duane L. Herrmann

Duane L. Herrmann, is a survivor who lived to tell, a writer who does not lie and a lover of the pure light of the moon - and trees! He is a contributor to the 2014 bestselling autobiographical anthology, *It's About Living.* He is also a 2010 Writers Matrix Award recipient, 2007 winner of the Ferguson Kansas History Book Award, 1989 Fellow of the Robert Hayden Poetry Fellowship, and is included in *American Poets of the 1990s, Kansas Poets Trail,* and *Map of Kansas Literature.* He has a variety of work published in four languages in a dozen countries and spends as much time as possible on his little piece of the rolling Kansas prairie reflected in *Prairies of Possibilities.*

♦   ♦   ♦

Madison Kallisti

Madison Kallisti is a reclusive creature, who occasionally ventures out during periods of manic frenzy, full of sound and fury, only to recede back into the subconscious when the sun rises.

◆　◆　◆

Jillian Koopman

Jillian Koopman is a 31 year-old writer and teacher living in Atlanta, Georgia. She is originally from Philadelphia, Pennsylvania. She attended Penn State University for a BA in English and Florida State University for an MFA in fiction writing. She enjoys reading, writing, cooking and exercising. Currently she teaches at Georgia Military College in Fairburn, Georgia, where she is an active part of student life. She is delighted to be included in this anthology.

◆　◆　◆

Thomas Krampf

Thomas Krampf's most recent work is *Selected Poems* with the essay "Perfecting the Art of Falling," (Salmon Poetry, 2012). He has read in universities, on NPR, and abroad. During the course of his writing career, he has both benefited and suffered from a schizophrenic-bi-polar disorder. Now recovered, he currently lives western NY in the Allegheny foothills with his wife, Françoise. They have three daughters and grandchildren.

◆　◆　◆

Craig Kurtz

Craig Kurtz lives at Twin Oaks Intentional Community where he writes poetry while simultaneously handcrafting hammocks. Recent work has appeared in *Bird's Thumb*, *The Bitchin Kitsch*, *BlazeVOX*, *B lotterature*, *Brev Spread*, *Drunk Monkeys*, *Leaves of Ink*, *Literati Quarterly*, *The Recusant*, *Three and a Half Point 9*, *Tower Journal*, and *Veil*.

◆　◆　◆

Savannah Logsdon-Breakstone

Savannah Logsdon-Breakstone is an Autistic queer femme with several disabilities. She writes at Cracked Mirror in Shalott (http://crackedmirrorinshalott.wordpress.com/) as well as contributing to other blogs, coordinates non-profit social media, and is an active disability rights advocate and activist . She lives in rural northwestern PA, USA with her dog.

Savannah's poetry may be also be found online at: http://nicocoer.blogspot.com/.

◆　◆　◆

V. Solomon Maday (ed.)

V. Solomon Maday began his love of music as a child and expanded his love of the arts to poetry after he met the editor-in-chief back in 2000. He is an Organist, accompanist, and choir director, beginning his career at age 16 when he started playing for a local church. He performed in many different venues in his late teens and early twenties, including a major production known as *Jhankar*, an Indian cultural program which featured local talent and spotlight artists. His recent interests include theology, science fiction, law, and philosophy. He lives in Grove City, Ohio with his fiancé.

◆   ◆   ◆

Chris McLean

Chris McLean is a Painter and Printmaker who lives in Santa Fe, New Mexico. His work focuses on the the immersion of the body in various energy forms; both natural and man made. He will be attending the Vermont Studio Center in January / February 2016 to work on a series of digital prints that re-mix Albrect Durer images with this concept in mind. He also plans on continuing the "SoundGardens" watercolor project, which translate the nuances of synaesthesia in a tangible visual manner.

◆   ◆   ◆

Laura Merleau

Laura Merleau received her doctoral degree in English from the University of Kansas in 2000. Since then, she has taught French, English Composition, and English as a Second Language at various universities in the Midwest. Her poetry has appeared in *Echolocation*, *Message in a Bottle*, and *Artistica*. She recently moved to Guangzhou, China, where she is teaching English at a private high school.

◆   ◆   ◆

David Mitchell

David Mitchell is Professor in the Department of English at George Washington University. He edits the "Corporealities: Discourses of Disability" scholarly book series for the University of Michigan Press, and with his partner, Sharon Snyder, he has co-authored three books, Narrative Prosthesis: Disability and the Dependencies of Discourse (U of Michigan P, 2001), Cultural Locations of Disability (U of Chicago P, 2006), and forthcoming, The Biopolitics of Disability: Neoliberalism, Ablenationalism, and Peripheral Embodiment (U of Michigan P, 2014). Back in 1997 he edited one of the inaugural collections of essays on disability history and representation, The Body and Physical Difference: Discourses of Disability (U of Michigan P, 1997), and since then has written more than 35 refereed journal essays and chapters on various aspects of disability culture, art, and history. He helped found the independent digital production company, Brace Yourselves Productions, and has produced 4 award winning documentary films: "Vital Signs: Crip Culture Talks Back" (1995); "A World Without Bodies" (2002); "Self Preservation: The Art of Riva Lehrer" (2004); and "Disability Takes on the Arts" (2005). David is currently working on a new book titled, Disability and Global Precarity.

A professional profile of David can be found here: http://english.columbian.gwu.edu/david-mitchell.

♦   ♦   ♦

Michael Scott Monje, Jr.

Michael is an Autonomous Press partner and the writer of multiple novels on the transgender autistic experience, including *Defiant, Mirror Project*, and the forthcoming *Imaginary Friends*. Her poetry has appeared in *Barking Sycamores, NeuroQueer*, and other venues, and a collection (*The US Book*) is forthcoming. Michael is also a member of The Puzzlebox Collective, where she is frequently called upon to read Athena's poetry aloud.

♦   ♦   ♦

N.I. Nicholson (ed.)

N.I. (Ian) Nicholson founded *Barking Sycamores* in early 2014. He also co-edited the 2015 *Spoon Knife Anthology* as well as the Summer 2014 Issue of *Red Wolf Journal*. Ian's poetry and essays have appeared in *NeuroQueer, GTK Creative Journal, Alphanumeric,* and *qarrtsiluni*. While pursuing an MFA in Creative Writing from Ashland University, he also blogs at The Digital Hyperlexic (http://thedigitalhyperlexic.wordpress.com/). He lives in Central Ohio with his fiancé and *Barking Sycamores* co-editor V. Solomon Maday. Ian is in the process of regenerating into his second incarnation.

◆ ◆ ◆

A.J. Odasso

A.J. Odasso's poetry has appeared in a number of strange and wonderful publications, including *Sybil's Garage*, *Mythic Delirium*, *Jabberwocky*, *Cabinet des Fées*, *Midnight Echo*, *Not One of Us*, *Dreams & Nightmares*, *Goblin Fruit*, *Strange Horizons*, *Stone Telling*, *Farrago's Wainscot*, *Through the Gate*, *Liminality*, *inkscrawl*, *Battersea Review*, and *SWAMP* (just to name a few). Her début collection, *Lost Books* (Flipped Eye Publishing, 2010), was nominated for the 2010 London New Poetry Award and for the 2011 Forward Prize, and was also a finalist for the 2011 People's Book Prize. Her second collection with Flipped Eye, *The Dishonesty of Dreams*, was released in August of 2014. Her two chapbooks, *Devil's Road Down* and *Wanderlust*, are available from Maverick Duck Press.   She has been serving as Senior Poetry Editor at *Strange Horizons* magazine since 2012.   She holds degrees from Wellesley College and the University of York (UK), and she is currently an MFA candidate and Teaching Fellow in Poetry at Boston University.

◆ ◆ ◆

Thomas Park

Thomas Park lives and teaches in Warrenton, North Carolina. He is developing the Warren County Artists Market (WAM), a non-profit writer's collective. Thomas views writing as a beautiful mode of self expression, and a means to advocate for the weak. He received a M.A. from Wayne State University in Detroit, and MFA from Goddard College,

Vermont. He has been published in *The Wayne Review*, *structural arc*, *West Trade Review*, and *Best New Poets*.

◆ ◆ ◆

C.F. Roberts

C.F. Roberts is a writer, visual artist, videographer and antimusician living on the Autism Spectrum in Northwest Arkansas with his wife, writer Heather Drain and a small menagerie of animals. He published and edited *SHOCKBOX: The Literary/Art Magazine with Teeth* from 1991 to 1996. He has numerous poetry, fiction and review publications to his credit, most recently in *Fearless*, *Gutter Eloquence*, *Paraphillia*, *Barking Sycamores*, *Pressure Press*, *Vagabonds: Anthology of the Mad Ones*, *Crab Fat Literary Magazine*, *The Birds We Piled Loosely*, *Blue Collar Review*, and *Antique Children*. His writing can be found at: http://cfrobertsuselessfilth.blogspot.com/. His artwork can also be found at: http://www.cfrobertsart.com/.

◆ ◆ ◆

Miss Roberts

Miss Roberts is an artist, illustrator and performer, she trained at The Slade School of Fine Art in London before rebelling, sticking on a wig, and telling weird and wonderful stories on stage. Since birth she has had strange episodes and hallucinations which were later diagnosed as epilepsy, these influence her story telling. She also illustrates beautiful hand made art books. Her blog can be read at http://themissroberts.wordpress.com.

◆ ◆ ◆

Maranda Russell

Maranda Russell is an award-winning author, artist, poet and blogger who also happens to have Asperger's Syndrome. She currently lives in Dayton, Ohio with her husband and six cats. For more information about this author or her books/artwork, please visit her website/blog, www.marandarussell.com.

◆ ◆ ◆

Barbara Ruth

Barbara Ruth is a housing justice warrior in Silicon Valley, a long time resident of California, a native of Kansas, an armchair traveler, and a lesbian everywhere she goes. *Barking Sycamores* is her artistic home. She looks forward to having a physical home of her own as well.

◆ ◆ ◆

Giorgia Sage

Giorgia Sage is a writer, San Francisco native, and is still not sure how she ended up in the middle of Connecticut, where she is studying Studio Art and Environmental Studies at Wesleyan University. Her poems have been published in *Your Impossible Voice*, *Sugar Mule*, *Girls Get Selfish*, and *The Found Poetry Review*, among other journals. Her work and various endeavors can be found on her website, giorgiasage.com and she herself can often be found crying on public transportation and moving worms off sidewalks during rainstorms.

◆ ◆ ◆

Phillip Sroka

Phillip Sroka was diagnosed bipolar (I) in 2007 at the age of 20. He has devoted his energies in a quasi-therapeutic devotion to his academic achievements. He earned a BA in philosophy with a minor in creative writing from the University of South Florida in 2012. He is currently pursuing from the same institution a Master's degree in English Rhetoric and Composition as well as a Master's in Library and Information Science which he expects to have both complete in 2016. Writing for Phil is the non plus ultra when it comes to coping with his afflictions and continues to be a vital part of his life. When he can he helps within the local art scenes to bring inclusion of divergent perspectives and representations of minority perspectives.

◆　　◆　　◆

Lucas Scheelk

Lucas Scheelk is a white, autistic, trans, queer-identified, mentally ill poet from the Twin Cities. Lucas uses "he, him, his" pronouns, and "they, them, their" pronouns. His work has appeared in publications such as *Sibling Rivalry Press - Assaracus, Glitterwolf Magazine, THEM - A Trans* Lit Journal, NonBinary Review*, among others. You can reach Lucas on twitter (@TC221Bee). Lucas is the author of *This Is A Clothespin* (Damaged Goods Press, 2016).

◆　　◆　　◆

A.D. Stone

Angelique, pen name A.D. Stone, has been writing poetry since she was a child, reading her first poem in front of her fourth grade class. Though she never stopped writing, she did stop sharing her words until 2009 when she discovered blogging and created a personal blog (Mindretrofit.com) in hopes of connecting with others who could relate to her journey of seeking understanding and acceptance. Since then, she has shared her Autism journey with her older son through writing, which led to her own diagnosis at the age of 39. In searching for a way to work through her emotions, she also created a poetry blog (mindretrofit7.wordpress.com) and has self-published four poetry books. Her writing delves into her love for words and wordplay; elucidating self-discoveries, exploring her personal traumas, untangling social confusion, fears, and anxieties, as well as offering a way to communicate and process living with synesthesia in such a sensory rich world.

♦ ♦ ♦

Bethany Tap

Bethany Tap is an MFA fiction candidate at the University of North Carolina in Wilmington. She does freelance work for *ideal-LIVING magazine* and is the managing editor of *Chautauqua*: the literary journal of the Chautauqua Institution.

♦ ♦ ♦

Jonathan Travelstead

Jonathan Travelstead served in the Air Force National Guard for six years as a firefighter and currently works as a full-time firefighter for the city of Murphysboro. Having finished his MFA at Southern Illinois University of Carbondale, he now works on an old dirt-bike he hopes will one day get him to the salt flats of Bolivia. He has published work in *The Iowa Review*, o n *Poetrydaily.com*, and has work forthcoming in *The Crab Orchard Review*, among others. His first collection *How We Bury Our Dead* by Cobalt/Thumbnail Press was released in March, 2015. His Facebook author's page can be found at: https://www.facebook.com/writerjonathantravelstead.

◆　◆　◆

Candy Waters

Candy Waters is a 15 year-old non-verbal autistic artist whose art has inspired people around the world. Candy's art has been featured in many places, including the cover of the Summer 2013 Issue of *University of California-Irvine Magazine* and on the cover of the 2013 Winter Issue of Something Special Magazine. Candy's art can be viewed and enjoyed on her Facebook page at: https://www.facebook.com/candywatersautismartist/

◆　◆　◆

Angela Weddle

Angela Weddle is a transgender visual artist and poet, who prefers to be called Alex, and who works in multiple media, primarily in pen and ink and watermedia. Weddle has Asperger's Syndrome,and Cerebral Palsy, is both self and formally taught, and is a local, national, and internationally exhibiting visual artist.

Weddle is originally from New Orleans, Louisiana and currently resides in San Antonio, TX.

◆   ◆   ◆

Christopher Wood-Robbins

Christopher Wood-Robbins, who prefers to be called "Aspie Chris" in his writings, lives in Central Massachusetts with his wife, Julie, and their tortoise-shell attack cat, Samantha. He often advocates for autism and Asperger acceptance at open mics just to "add another shade to the rainbow of diversity."